MW00827607

Trust *in*
the Future

BOOKS BY BASTIAAN BAAN

The Chymical Wedding of Christian Rosenkreutz:
A Commentary on a Christian Path of Initiation

Lord of the Elements:
Interweaving Christianity and Nature

Old and New Mysteries:
From Trials to Initiation

Sources of Christianity:
Peter, Paul and John

Sources of Religious Worship:
A History of Ritual from the Stone Age to the Present Day

Ways into Christian Meditation

Trust *in* the Future

Facing Uncertain Times with Confidence

BASTIAAN BAAN

with contributions by Jesse Mulder

Floris Books

Translated by Philip Mees

First published in Dutch as *Toekomst van de Aarde*
by Christofoor Publishers, Netherlands in 2022
First published in English by Floris Books, Edinburgh in 2024
© 2022 Uitgeverij Christofoor
English version © 2024 Floris Books

All rights reserved. No part of this book may
be reproduced without prior permission of
Floris Books, Edinburgh
www.florisbooks.co.uk

 Also available as an eBook

British Library CIP data available
ISBN 978-178250-919-6

Contents

Contents

Foreword

Nothing is more unpredictable than the future of humanity and the earth on which we live. Although countless generations and cultures have tried to predict the near and distant future, we should accept the fact that usually these visions are either puzzling and hard to interpret or sometimes completely beside the truth. Every so often, our so-called experts make strong predictions about future developments, but past results are no guarantee of what the future will bring. For example, according to President Harry Truman, when Fleet Admiral William Leahy heard of U.S. efforts to create the atomic bomb, he responded, 'The atomic bomb will never go off. I speak as an expert in explosives.'[1]

Not only down-to-earth expertise, but also clairvoyance is not enough to predict the future, as long as it remains clouded by subjective wishes and emotions. When Rudolf Steiner was once asked about predicting the future, he answered, 'This is possible, but the occultist refrains from doing so, because, almost always, it behoves only a high initiate to know the future. The initiate's prevision does not determine what another person does; the latter will act in the future entirely out of his free will.'[2] In other words, even the few initiates who are able to perceive the future have to withhold their knowledge so that others will not be influenced by them.

Instead of trying to predict the future, or even develop different scenarios for it, this book focuses most of all on our attitude to events that come towards us. The nineteenth-century philosopher Wilhelm von Humboldt once expressed the quality that is needed to stand firm in life as follows: 'It is almost more important how a person takes his fate than what it is.' When we are unable to change circumstances and events, we either become a puppet of fate or we are challenged to change ourselves – beginning with the way we view our destiny. Is it possible to develop trust in our future, even if the perspective appears unfavourable or outright disastrous? This is the approach that I wish to share with readers in this book.

Despite the fact that it is impossible to predict the future in detail, my aim in this book is to describe current trends and developments that are leading us into the future. At the same time, I attempt to interpret the imaginative language of some prophetic books, although it is not easy to understand this language. With these tools, however, it is possible to develop at least an inkling of what comes towards us from the future.

Bastiaan Baan

1

Signs of the Times

The future depends on what you do today.

Mahatma Gandhi

When people take a trip to another country they usually prepare in advance, often looking in a travel guide for interesting places to visit, sometimes planning their trips down to the smallest details, so that little or nothing is left to chance. This was not the case in the past, however. Explorers would travel to what they called *terra incognita*, meaning 'unknown land', not knowing what was waiting for them there. For such a trip they could not devise a detailed itinerary; they had to be prepared for anything. Nowadays when something unexpected occurs, we fall back on the well-known saying, 'Life is what happens while you are making other plans.'

This is the picture I have of humanity as we journey into the future. There is no map, no clearly determined route. Don't expect any predictions in this book that are set in stone declaring that things are going to happen a particular way and only this way. That is even more true for our time than for the past.

It is one of the signs of our time that we live in a world that is constantly changing, or, as we might also say, we live in a world where the only certainty is uncertainty. That is also the theme of a book written by sociologist and philosopher Zygmunt Bauman, called *Liquid Modernity*. We used to call something modern when it was the very latest, or when the product had been developed to a state of perfection. These days 'modern' is taken to be an infinity of improvements, in which there is no longer any static condition, but never-ending change and a perpetual search for renewal. That is liquid modernity.

In times past, people used to speak of 'providence', referring to that authority that was able to see what would happen in the future (from the Latin *pro-videre*, meaning to foresee). In religious terms, the future is an open book only for God. Watch out, therefore, for the fortune tellers who tell you the world is going to end on a particular date. There were many who said the world would end on January 1, 2000, and yet we are still here. But perhaps it is going to pass away on January 1, 2026? I know people who profess that and swear that it is so, and yet if people like them were right then the world would have passed away a thousand times already. Of course, these fortune tellers have a thousand excuses: 'God felt sorry for us and changed his plans again.'

Clairvoyance is not clear enough to see the future in all its aspects. Initiates can sometimes read the hidden causes behind outer events, but they are unable to see the future in its entirety. Rudolf Steiner expressed this in one of his so-called mystery dramas. In *The Soul's Awakening*, the initiate Benedictus recognises images of the future and says: 'This I can sense. How it will come to pass remains a secret hidden from my sight.'[1]

Even Christ himself, during his life on earth, was unable to see the future in its totality. In the Little Apocalypse, which we will look at in a later chapter, he said:

> Heaven and earth will pass away, but my words will not pass away. No one knows anything about that day or that hour, not even the angels in heaven, nor the Son, but only the Father.
> (Mark 13:31-32)

When we read the mythologies of various peoples, and religious texts like the Little Apocalypse and the Apocalypse of St John, we encounter a language of images. This imagery is in itself an open secret, something that still has to be deciphered, and while it is susceptible to various interpretations, it nevertheless points in a certain direction. Even though we don't speak the language of myths and prophecies anymore, countless people live with indeterminate feelings about the future. We sometimes speak of a 'sixth sense', and we all know expressions like 'It's in the air' or 'Something casts its shadow ahead of it'. But it is only shadows, nothing tangible that can allow us to recognise what will take place in the future.

In his book *Theory U*, the German academic and author Otto Scharmer[2] developed a method of what he called 'leading from the future as it emerges'. A group of people, entrepreneurs for example, deliberate together and try to develop a sense for what is coming towards them from the future.

All too often, however, we are way off the mark and are blind to the potential the future offers us. In our time – perhaps more than ever before – we constantly alternate between hope and fear, between the most extreme forms of despair and pessimism, and blind hope and trust.

The reality of our time is made even more complicated because we are threatened by what is sometimes called the 'infocalypse': an overwhelming, destructive chaos of information. These days we not only have to do with reality as it happens around us, but also with a distorted reality that is produced by both traditional media and online social media. We are living in a 'post-truth' era, where people are more willing to believe what they feel about something than the facts relating to it.[3] We cannot simply trust our observations. The illusions created by the various media, including 'deep fake' technologies, are already so realistic that very soon we will no longer be able to distinguish truth from appearance. Through refined technology truth and lie will be manipulated into their opposites. Politicians who want to stay informed about the latest developments not only need the help of information experts, but also of disinformation experts: professionals who focus on the art of distinguishing reality from appearance. In the face of such bewildering complexity, many people turn to conspiracy theories for simple answers.

In his book *The End of the Middle*, Farid Tabarki describes the extremes in which our society finds itself caught today. He points out that what used to hold these extremes together, the more moderate middle ground, is disappearing. We are familiar with this not only in society and politics, and in relationships between people, but also in nature, which increasingly is speaking to us through extreme phenomena. To an important extent this is the result of human activity. This was made clear in the short film *Anthropocence*, which opened the United Nations Conference on Sustainable Development in Rio de Janeiro in 2012. The documentary travels through the history of the past 250 years in three minutes, starting with the Industrial Revolution. Before that time there had been a long period of relative stability lasting around 12,000 years known as the Holocene. According to the makers of this film, however, since the beginning of the Industrial Revolution we can no longer speak of the Holocene. Instead, we must refer to this period as the Anthropocene, which denotes the period of time in which human beings have become the decisive factor in the future of the earth.

There is an old saying: 'Humanity proposes, God disposes,' which means that while people can make plans, ultimately it is God who decides how things will turn out. Increasingly, however, it seems we are saying the opposite: God proposes, humanity disposes. God makes plans, but in the end, it is up to humanity how things will turn out. This is because we are no longer marionettes in God's hands, puppets in a drama in which, at the decisive moment, God descends to the earth to put everything right, in dramatic terms known as *Deus ex machina*. God has withdrawn from creation and no longer works directly into humanity; he is no longer the single determining factor.

This idea has been strikingly expressed in a poem called *Waiting for a Miracle*:

I heard that many of you are waiting for a miracle,
The miracle that I, your God, would save the world.

How can I save without your help?
How can I speak without your voice?
How can I love without your hearts?
From the seventh day I have given everything out
    of my hands,
My whole creation, all my power.
Not you, but I am now waiting for a miracle.

Maybe the author, who is unknown to me, received their inspiration for this poem from the principal person in this poem.

There was a time when human beings were like marionettes, pulled on the strings of the Godhead. In ancient Egypt, the people were the marionettes of the Pharaoh, and the Pharaoh the marionette of the Godhead. The Godhead worked in and through the Pharaoh; the Pharaoh worked in and through the people. But the people had no voice of their own, they did not yet have their own individuality. During the course of our development human beings have detached themselves from their origin, but this brought with it a certain hardening. In the Old Testament, for example, Yahweh complains to the prophets about human beings, saying: 'Their hearts are like stone' (see, for example, Ezekiel 36:26). The human heart, which was once receptive to the voice of God, has hardened, it has closed itself off from the inspiration of the Godhead. This is tragic, but also necessary.

In the world we inhabit between death and rebirth, we are not free; we are bound to the consequences of our deeds. If we have hurt someone during life on earth, then after death we have to put ourselves in their place and inwardly experience what our words and deeds have done to them. But here on earth, we are able to act the way our heart, our head, or our desires move us. As has already been mentioned, this is because from the beginning of creation the Godhead has given us more and more room to unfold our own activity. The Kabbalah, the Jewish mystical tradition, has a special word for this exceptional deed of the Godhead: *tzimtzum*. What is *tzimtzum*? It is the divine art of constraint. According to the Kabbalah, God not only placed his creation outside of himself (in philosophy this process is called emanation), but he also made an opposite movement. God withdrew and, in creating human beings, he gave latitude to opposing powers, which are also his creations.

Anthroposophy describes a number of adversarial beings that humanity must deal with during the course of its evolution. One such being is Ahriman, the name given to Satan in ancient Persia. Ahriman and the beings that follow him want to chain us to the earth and obscure our view of the future, making us forever fearful and threatening us with paralysis. Another being is Lucifer, who wants to cloud our consciousness and lead us away from the earth into a make-believe world of bliss and beauty. There is also a third category of beings, known as the Asuras, who inspire terror and destruction through various groups and governments around the world. They want to bring disaster upon the earth, a word that literally means 'without a star': dis-aster. Heaven is completely banished. This all leads to total nihilism.

As ominous as this all sounds, it is a necessary condition for human beings to develop freedom. In their paradisal condition human beings were like little children, and, like all children who rebel against their parents as they become increasingly independent, humanity rebelled against the Godhead. You might say that humanity is currently going through its adolescent phase for the purpose of no longer being children of God, but instead becoming fully grown-up sons and daughters of God.

The apostle Paul was the first to introduce this concept into the history of humanity. In his Letter to the Romans, he writes about the spirit of sonship. Human beings have received a spirit that wants to help them no longer be children, but to become sons and daughters of God: 'The creation waits in eager expectation for the sons of God to be revealed' (Rom. 8:19).

Paul indicates in this text that the whole creation, which is no longer under the care of the angelic hierarchies, looks expectantly to human beings. In a certain sense, the creation has been given into the hands of human beings since God withdrew from it, and now it is waiting for the redeeming word of the sons and daughters of God. This is, you might say, the religious expression of the concept of the Anthropocene. Paul created a new word for this: *huiothesia*, which is translated as 'sonship' (literally it means 'placing the son', from *hyiós*, meaning 'son' and *títhēmi*, meaning 'to place'). Unfortunately, Luther did not dare translate that concept as 'the sons of God', and thus wrongly translated it as 'the children of God'.

When we look to the future we find in the Apocalypse of St John a striking expression of the human being as an independent, self-contained personality: 'I stand at the door and knock. If anyone hears my voice and opens the door, I will come in and eat with him, and he with me' (Rev. 3:20). Christ, who plays a key role in the future of the earth, stops before the door that separates us from him and knocks; he does not enter without our permission: 'If anyone hears my voice and opens the door, I will come in.' Nor does it suffice for us just to hear his voice (Rudolf Steiner spoke of the voice of Christ as the voice of human conscience), we have to act accordingly and open the door of our closed-up personality to him. Then there follows an enigmatic statement. When we think of the meal of Christ, we always think of the one who gives us the meal, but apparently, we also have to give something to him and 'eat with him, and he with me'. Only in this combination of giving and receiving does true communion grow.

I am ending this introductory chapter with a quotation from a lecture by Rudolf Steiner, words that could be the motto of this book. It is a fragment from a lecture given in Bremen on November 27, 1910. This quotation does not tell us what will happen in the future, but gives us the instrument to develop confidence for the future:

> We must eradicate from the soul all fear and terror of what comes to man out of the future.

15

We must acquire serenity in all feelings and sensations
    about the future.

We must look forward with absolute equanimity
    to all that may come,
And we must think only that whatever comes
Is given to us by a world direction full of wisdom.
It is part of what we must learn in this age, namely
    to live out of pure trust,
Without any security in existence,
Trust in the ever-present help of the spiritual world.
Truly, nothing else will do.
Let us discipline our will, let us seek the awakening
    from within ourselves
Every morning and every evening.[4]

I will come back to this text later in the book, but for now it allows us to recognise what providence truly is: wise leading powers that not only see what is going to happen, but also foresee how humanity can be helped in all circumstances according to the principle: 'Help yourself, so help you God.' Similarly, in a lecture to the future priests of The Christian Community, and in what we can see as an appeal to our courage as well as theirs, Rudolf Steiner said: 'It might be that in the future humanity will go through an abyss. The only thing people can do then is to go through the abyss and come up again on the other side.'

2

What Do Mythologies
Say About the Future?

The primary function of mythology is to awaken a feeling in the individual human being of respect and wonder, and to let him feel part of the unfathomable mystery of being.

Joseph Campbell

You will have noticed from the previous chapter that this book does not give ready-made answers to the question of what the future holds for us. Whoever is expecting that will be disappointed. To put it even more strongly, I am convinced that ready-made answers are illusions. The future is not cut in stone, it is in our hands – which means it is not only in the hands of God. It would be an illusion to make God responsible for all that we are doing to the earth, as if it were his fault that we ruthlessly exploit its resources on a huge scale.

At the same time, we must realise that we are not the only ones who have the destiny of the earth in our hands. Ancient mythologies speak in many different ways of a God or gods who bear and order, create and destroy, life on earth. In our demythologising time we, too, are forced to acknowledge greater powers than those of human beings – if it is only the power of nature, which most of the time has the last word (see the concept of 'panarchy' discussed in Chapter 11).

Before we look for answers to the question of what mythologies say about the future, it is necessary to understand what myths, mythologies and mythical consciousness are. The Greek word *mythos* means several things relating to speech, such as a tale or a story. Plato was one of the first to use the word 'mythology', which is composed of the words *mythos* and *logos* – story and word or concept. In Plato's time the word *mythos* began to acquire a different meaning, one that we recognise today: fiction, fantasy, a fable.

Plato, however, continued to use the word in its original meaning. According to him, myths are inspirations of the initiates, the *mystai*. They are symbolic images, inspirations in the original meaning of this word, meaning that the gods inspired the initiates to write the myths. In his dialogue *Phaedrus*, a conversation about the soul, Plato indicates what misunderstandings had arisen during his time about myths. In *Phaedrus*, the myth of Boreas, the god of the wind, is told. Boreas falls in love with Orithya, the daughter of an Attic king. Boreas abducts her and imprisons her in a cave.

Contemporaries of Plato responded by saying, 'That is indeed the story of the daughter of this Attic king, but she was standing on a cliff by the sea; a gust of wind came and threw her into the sea. She fell from the cliff.' But Plato, through the mouthpiece of his former teacher, Socrates, writes:

> I regard such theories as no doubt attractive, but as the invention of clever, industrious people who are not exactly to be envied, for the simple reason that they must then go on and tell us the real truth about the appearance of Centaurs and the Chimera.

He then adds something very interesting to this myth:

> [I] direct my enquiries ... to myself, to discover whether I really am a more complex creature and more puffed up with pride than Typhon.[1]

Myths do not describe the physical world, but an inner world where outer observations and pictures no longer exist.

In the past century and a half, a variety of views about myths have developed, ranging from allegories to remainders of rituals, personifications, or fantasies of historical events. The nineteenth-century philosopher Max Müller saw the origin of myths in natural phenomena and viewed the birth of the gods as 'a disease of the language'.[2] A natural phenomenon, which originally merely had a name (such as the sun), became a god (Helios).

An exception to this naturalistic view of what a myth is lies in the work of the writer and professor of literature Joseph Campbell, who recognised universal patterns in myths. He compared the myths of various peoples, cultures and time periods in his book *The Hero with a Thousand Faces*, and was also influenced by the views of Carl Gustav Jung who believed that myths, legends and stories about gods and heroes contained archetypal images that lived in the collective unconscious of humanity.

This also resonates with what Rudolf Steiner spoke of in a lecture he gave in Prague on April 17, 1914, namely that myths and fairy tales have their origin in the spiritual world, in the imaginations and inspirations of initiates. Myths and fairy tales can help human beings recognise the light of the spiritual world in their own soul. Like connects with like. Steiner, like many of his contemporaries, described how myths and fairy tales arose in the childhood of humanity. People at that time were in a certain sense like children but, according to Steiner, they were instructed by the gods. In this lecture he connected this view with something that is still true today:

In the process of our evolution, myths and fairy tales are gradually lost, but children should not grow up without them. It makes a tremendous difference whether or not children are allowed to grow up with fairy tales. The power of the fairy tale images, which give wings to the soul, becomes apparent only at a later age. Growing up without fairy tales leads later to boredom, to world-weariness.[3]

The imagery of fairy tales speaks sometimes of 'bread that never runs out'. The hero of the story receives bread that keeps replenishing itself. Similarly, you could say that myths and fairy tales are an inexhaustible source of nourishment for the life of the soul, even after death.

When I was a teacher in a Waldorf school in the 1970s, I had the direct experience of how myth fell on fertile ground with children who, consciously or half consciously, recognised the archetypal images contained in them. I was telling my fourth-grade pupils stories from Germanic mythology found in the Edda. The beginning of the Edda describes in enigmatic, complicated imagery the beginning of the world and the many gods that bring the creation into existence. As I was preparing the lesson, I wondered whether I should be telling this story to children of nine and ten, and yet when I came to the end a girl said, 'Yes, that is how I used to think that the world was made.' For her and her contemporaries the pictures were quite natural. We adults, on the other hand, are often hindered by intellectual obstacles. In a parents' meeting one evening, I related how the children responded to the story. Upon hearing this, one of the parents, a clever engineer, grumbled, 'I don't understand why children these days have to listen to such cowboy stories.'

Again, this resonates with something Steiner said in another lecture in which he related images from myths and fairy tales to our time. He explained that while so-called down-to-earth people would really like to exclude education through fairy tales, myths and legends, children are born with these imaginations:

For what is seated deep within the child's soul are the imaginations that have been received in the spiritual world. They seek to come to the surface. The teacher or the educator adopts the right attitude towards the child if he confronts the child with pictures. By placing images before the child's soul, there flash up from its soul those images, or, strictly speaking, those forces of pictorialised representation which have been received before birth or, let us say, prior to conception.

Steiner then described the opposite of this. What is the result when adults no longer want to give this content to children, and when their upbringing and education consist exclusively of intellectual and practical schooling? What is the result when these images are kept away from children? He said:

> What kind of people will come into being from that? They will
> be rebels, revolutionaries, dissatisfied people; people who do
> not know what they want, because they want something that
> one cannot know. This is because they want something that
> is incompatible with any possible social order ... Therefore,
> we can say that people who, in an occult sense, do not have
> honest intentions in regard to their fellowmen, do not have
> the courage to admit to themselves: 'If the world is in a state
> of revolt today, it is really heaven that is revolting.' It means
> the heaven that is held back in the souls of individuals, which
> then comes to the fore, not in its own form, but in its opposite
> – in strife and bloodshed instead of imaginations. No wonder
> that the individuals who destroy the social fabric actually have
> the feeling that they are doing good. For what do they sense
> in themselves? They feel heaven within themselves; only it
> assumes the form of a caricature in their soul.[4]

I myself have experienced what happens when mythical images you pick up as a child, and which lead a slumbering existence, suddenly come to life again at a decisive moment. I was seventeen when my father died unexpectedly, and I received the news without any preparation. When the message of his passing reached me, it was as if I lost the ground under my feet. In the chaos of emotions and memories that washed over me, the beginning of a verse came to mind that I had learned as a child in a Waldorf school:

Gilgamesh, King of Uruk
Reigned as a divine hero.
Among human beings
He could not find his equal...[5]

The Babylonian epic of *Gilgamesh*, which we had drummed into our memory in the fifth grade, is the first myth of gods and humans in which death is described as a riddle. When Gilgamesh's dearest friend, Enkidu, dies, Gilgamesh is no longer able to reach him in the land of the dead. The natural connection that had existed between the living and the dead by then is broken. Although I had long since forgotten the words and images of this myth, at this moment they rose up in me and gave meaning to my first confrontation with death. Instead of being thrown back onto myself, I felt a connection with that profound experience.

Myths show us where we come from and where we are going, both individually and collectively. Comparisons of myths in different cultures show that practically all of them describe a pure, original creation that is disrupted by lower gods who have turned away from the Creator. Although human beings were created by God, we were seduced by these fallen gods into original sin, which subsequently spread over the whole paradisal creation.

Among the oldest myths we possess are the Indian Vedas. The word *veda* literally means 'knowing' or 'knowledge'. According to tradition, the Vedas are *shruti*, meaning they were revealed to seers. For centuries they were handed down orally from one generation to the next, until around 1500 BC they were written down. The Vedas describe a cycle of creations. To begin with there is an original, pure creation, which then becomes corrupted, prompting the Godhead to destroy the world. The creation passes over into *pralaya*, a kind of cosmic sleep in which everything is taken back up into the Godhead. Out of this *pralaya* a new creation arises.

A similar picture presents itself to us in the Old Testament. The book of Genesis describes how humanity turns away from its origin and, with an all-too-human expression, how God suffers under the original sin of humanity:

> The Lord saw how great the wickedness of the human race
> had become on the earth, and that every inclination of the
> thoughts of the human heart was only evil all the time.
> The Lord regretted that he had made human beings on the
> earth, and his heart was deeply troubled. (Gen. 6:5–6)

In these remarkable words we are shown how, from divine grief, divine wrath could be born. God decides to destroy the creation, which leads to the story of the Great Flood.

There is an interesting difference, however, between earlier and later myths across different cultures. To demonstrate this, I will take a few brief examples from the ancient Indian Mahabharata, and Greek, Jewish and Christian myths. What do these myths tell us about the future? The Mahabharata and the Puranas describe a creation that is destroyed by a world conflagration when seven suns scorch the earth. The fire of the cosmos annihilates everything on earth and in heaven. The earth is then inundated by twelve years of rain, during which the god Vishnu, who is sitting on the cosmic serpent Sesha, falls asleep. In the *pralaya* that follows, the Godhead again takes back his creation. He breathes his creation in until Vishnu wakes up in the form of *prana*[6] in a new creation. The remarkable aspect of this epic is that in this series of creation, development, destruction and *pralaya* followed by a new creation, the human being plays hardly any role. We are still in the initial phase of humanity: everything is still in the hands of God.

This changes in Greek mythology, where the destruction of the earth is the result of the degeneration of humanity. The fifth-century BC philosopher Heraclitus describes the end of the old creation by fire. Plato describes the destruction of the previous creation by a great flood that submerges Atlantis.[7] In Greek mythology human beings appear from time to time as opposing the Godhead. Think of the figure of Prometheus who steals fire from heaven. Human beings begin to lead a life of their own and, in doing so, anger the gods.

In Jewish mythology, despite the collective destruction of humanity, the individual for the first time begins to play a role. In its writings, Jewish culture speaks of the judgment of the individual according to his or her deeds. We will come back to this in the chapters on the Little Apocalypse and the Apocalypse of St John (see chapters 4 and 5).

In these brief descriptions we see how the myths develop from showing human beings in the hands of the Godhead to them obstinately resisting the divine world. If we turn once again to the Edda, we find that not only does German mythology describe the destruction of the world but also, and this is new in mythology, the destruction of the world of the gods. Here we witness the downfall of the entire creation.

Ragnarök, or Twilight of the Gods as it is also known, begins with a winter that lasts for three years and spreads across the whole earth. This cold is the result of strife among people: nature reflects back the consequences of human deeds, something that is becoming ever more apparent in our secularised world. In mythical form, the Edda describes how human beings and demons drag the creation down with them in their fall. Humanity has forgotten the gods and war arises among people, a war of all against all:

> Brothers shall fight, and fell each other,
> And sisters' sons shall kinship strain;
> Hard is it on earth, with mighty whoredom;
> Wind-time, wolf-time, ere the world falls;
> Nor ever shall men each other spare.

The gods are pulled into the destruction that is begun by humanity and the powers of evil. The gods are attacked by their own creatures. The Fenris Wolf devours the sun, and the moon is destroyed; the stars fall from heaven, the earth trembles, and the gods go to war against the demons. To the horror of the seeress who describes these pictures, evil appears stronger than good. Gods are being killed by their opponents. Then the silent god, Vidar, steps forward. He had held back during the preceding creation and now he kills the Fenris Wolf. He inserts his right foot into the wolf's wide-open muzzle and tears it in two. The Völva, the seeress, describing what she sees, says: 'Up I see rising once again green earth from the sea.' From the war of all against all a new creation arises. One human pair, Liv and Livtrasi, who were preserved in the wood of a tree like seeds, form the beginning of a new creation.

Yet even more mysterious than Vidar is the god of the gods, whose name may not be mentioned. He judges and restores the creation; gods and humans return.

Wherever you look in ancient mythologies, the end of the world, the destruction of the creation, is at the same time the beginning of a new creation. But over the course of the centuries the emphasis changes. In the oldest theocracies the Godhead is the active agent who asserts its omnipotence, whereas in later times human beings increasingly become the decisive factor in events. In the Old Testament this is expressed in one of the psalms: 'The heavens are the Lord's heavens, but the earth he has given to the sons of men' (Ps. 115:16).

3

Old Forms of Predicting the Future: Prophets, Sibyls and Shamans

The engulfing waters threatened me, the deep surrounded me;
seaweed was wrapped around my head. To the roots of the
mountains I sank down; the earth beneath barred me in forever.
But you, Lord my God, brought my life up from the pit.

Jonah 2:5–6

Large numbers of people today suffer from doom-laden thoughts about the future, or else they attempt to escape into illusory ideas about an imagined utopia they believe will come about any day now. These fears and illusions are not only unnecessary, they also present the biggest obstacle to facing the future honestly and objectively. It is well known from psychology that hopelessness, aimlessness and loss of meaning ruin our quality of life and disturb our view of the here and now.

In ancient cultures people turned to particular individuals for guidance in their lives and for insight into the future. These individuals played an important role in society and were often consulted on coming events. Indeed, in our age of uncertainty we can hardly imagine what a society under their leadership must have looked like. But the priests and prophets of those times helped people understand their present circumstances by reminding them of their origins and giving them a glimpse of the future.

We can recognise this threefoldness of past, present and future in the composition of many classic myths and legends. They begin with the creation of the world, then go on to describe the evolution of humanity, and end with a view of the future. We see the same kind of composition in the Old Testament, where a distinction is usually made between the historical books, the poetic books and the prophetic books. The historical books go back to Genesis and the creation of the world; they give a bird's eye view of the history of humanity, and of the Jewish people in particular. The psalms are poetry, a record of individual human beings responding to their destiny and that of their people. Finally, the Old Testament prophets provide insight into the future.

In the New Testament this threefoldness may be recognised in the four Gospels and the Acts of the Apostles (historical books), the letters of the various apostles (poetic books) and the Book of Revelation. In this threefoldness we see three different ways in which the spiritual world reveals itself. The historical books contain imaginations; the spiritual world expresses itself in images. In the poetic books inspiration is the source; the spiritual world expresses itself to the inner, spiritual ear through the musical quality of the psalms and poems. Finally, the spiritual world reveals itself to prophets and the author of the Apocalypse in imagination, inspiration *and* intuition. In intuition the spiritual world not only becomes visible (imagination), and audible (inspiration), but also becomes a tangible experience. The prophet Isaiah is touched with fire from the heavenly altar, so that his lips are cleansed (Isa. 6:7). John has to 'eat' the touch of the spiritual world, so that his inner being becomes bitter (Rev.10:10).

These scriptures were guidelines for a whole culture, and the same is true for countless texts that form the foundations of other cultures. They create an awareness of our origin and future. If we have no idea of history and how we fit into that history, then we can only live in the dark from one day to the next. When we lose the knowledge of our past, we drift into the future without any goal or perspective, and this is what creates fear and anxiety.

In this chapter I will describe and compare three different traditions found in the ancient world that were concerned with predicting the future: the prophetic, sibylline and shamanic traditions. They come from an era when human beings had a very different relationship with the world of the spirit and with the future, and as such may not be considered appropriate for people of today.

The prophets

The era of the prophets began around the eighth century BC and ended without a trace around two hundred years later. It was a period of chaos marked by the Assyrian and Babylonian captivities. The state of Israel fell apart and was destroyed, and the Jewish people spread over the area around the Mediterranean in the diaspora. They became 'homeless'.

The Old Testament prophets were the exponents of this pre-Christian era. But they did not limit themselves to lamenting the tragedy of Israel's downfall; they also showed the way up out of the way down and how the spiritual world can break through a culture that, in its outer manifestation, is perishing. In this sense, prophets of doom were also prophets of salvation: in the turbulence of their times they recognised the signs of the coming Messiah. A number of the prophets even looked beyond this future time to a far more distant future. Long before the Apocalypse of St John, the prophets Ezekiel and Isaiah wrote about a new heaven and a new earth (see Ezekiel chapters 40 to 48, and Isaiah 65:17–25).

For the prophet Daniel the experience of the coming calamity and the salvation following it is even more urgent than for his predecessors. Daniel was the first to write about the culmination of evil in a distant future. He used an expression we also encounter in the Little Apocalypse found in the Gospels of Matthew, Mark and Luke, one that may be translated as 'desolating sacrilege' or 'abomination causing desolation'. The Greek text shows a different nuance: *to bdelugma tès eremōseōs*. In the word *eremōseōs* we recognise the word for hermit, *erimìtis*, as well as *éremos*, which means desert or loneliness. Daniel was describing a future in which humanity would be divided and each person would be thrown back onto themselves. But he also had a concrete picture that became a historical reality just a few centuries later. He foresaw a time when the Jewish temple would be taken over by the Roman Caesars who would proclaim themselves to be gods and set their statues in the Holy of Holies. This is the 'desolating sacrilege'.

Thus, in dramatic imagery, the prophets showed how increasing depravity, inner hardening and the influence of demonic forces would increase like shadows cast by a great light – the light of the coming Messiah. This is something that happens in all time periods, but we are often so obsessed with the shadows that we have become blind to the light.

In our own time we often have the tendency to be preoccupied with decadence and destruction. The more we look for support in the material world, the more hopeless our time and future may seem. The prophets, however, teach us to look beyond the misery. For the thoughtful reader, their prophecies – and this also holds true for the Little Apocalypse and the Apocalypse of St John – are means to overcome fear of the future. Daniel wrote, 'There will be a time of distress such as has not happened from the beginning of nations' (Dan. 12:1), but always his view was to persevere, to continue on and look past the fear and darkness.

In some of the writings of the prophets, we see how a person becomes a prophet. Isaiah gives an impressive description of his own calling. In his imagination one of the Seraphim shows him the trial by fire that a human being has to go through in order to become a prophet. Isaiah enters the spiritual world where the throne of God appears before his inner eye. The curtain of the temple tears open and he sees the heavenly cult of which all earthly rituals are a reflection. He beholds what is often called the Sanctus of the Seraphim: the highest regions of the hierarchies, the realm of the Seraphim, who unceasingly celebrate their heavenly cult:

In the year that King Uzziah died, I saw the Lord, high and exalted, seated on a throne; and the train of his robe filled the temple. Above him were seraphim, each with six wings: With two wings they covered their faces, with two they covered their feet, and with two they were flying. And they were calling to one another: 'Holy, holy, holy is the Lord Almighty; the whole earth is full of his glory.' At the sound of their voices the doorposts and thresholds shook and the temple was filled with smoke. (Isa. 6:1-4)

This threefold 'holy' or Sanctus relates to the worship of the Trinity, which was called by the Church Father Dionysius the Areopagite[1] 'the theology of the Seraphim'.

Isaiah describes what happens next:

'Woe to me!' I cried. 'I am ruined! For I am a man of unclean lips, and I live among a people of unclean lips, and my eyes have seen the King, the Lord Almighty.' Then one of the seraphim flew to me with a live coal in his hand, which he had taken with tongs from the altar. With it he touched my mouth and said, 'See, this has touched your lips; your guilt is taken away and your sin atoned for.' Then I heard the voice of the Lord saying, 'Whom shall I send? And who will go for us?' And I said, 'Here am I. Send me! Send me.' (Isa. 6:5–8)

Only now has Isaiah become a prophet. He had to be touched with heavenly fire by the highest hierarchies. Readers who are familiar with the service of the Consecration of the Human Being in The Christian Community will recognise this passage in the preparation of the Gospel reading where the priest says: 'My heart be filled with Your pure life, o Christ. From my lips let flow the word purified by You.' The Gospel must not be read but proclaimed. Rudolf Steiner once said to the priests of The Christian Community: 'On the "worthily"

depends an extraordinary amount in the conception of the priest ...
In this wrestling for worthiness to fulfil the Mass lies the divestment
of the personal.'[2]

The ego has to enter the crucible in order to speak supra-personally,
supra-humanly. The calling of Isaiah was a paragon of prophecy in
which all that is personal became the bearer of a supra-personal being.

At this point Isaiah receives the task to prophesy:

'Go and tell this people: "Be ever hearing, but never
understanding; be ever seeing, but never perceiving." Make
the heart of this people calloused; make their ears dull and
close their eyes. Otherwise they might see with their eyes, hear
with their ears, understand with their hearts, and turn and be
healed.' Then I said, 'For how long, Lord?' And he answered:
'Until the cities lie ruined and without inhabitant, until the
houses are left deserted and the fields ruined and ravaged, until
the Lord has sent everyone far away and the land is utterly
forsaken. And though a tenth remains in the land, it will again
be laid waste. But as the terebinth and oak leave stumps when
they are cut down, so the holy seed will be the stump in the
land.' (Isa. 6:9–13)

The last thing you would expect a prophet's task to be is to close
the hearts, eyes and ears of the people, and yet this is exactly what
God asks Isaiah to do. This is because the time has now come for
human beings to become 'closed' personalities, to let go of the old
clairvoyance that in ancient times meant people were still receptive
to inspiration from God. From Isaiah's time on, however, atavism is
an evolutionary dead-end: the old must be let go. The 'stump' that
remains is the sobering quality of thinking, the abstract intellect, and
it becomes the task of the Jewish people to develop this.

With the development of the intellect, human beings have become
hermits. We no longer feel connected with everything and to everyone;

we have been thrown back onto ourselves. You could say that what the Jewish people went through as pioneers has subsequently become the common property of humanity: that is the necessary stage of isolation, which leads to loneliness.

Dag Hammarskjöld, Secretary General of the United Nations in the 1950s, once wrote: 'Lonely, but loneliness can also be communion.' In his diary he shares with his reader a loneliness that becomes transparent to a reality that transcends the personal ego. Necessary loneliness is the true reason why we so often find the prophets in the desert. As has already been mentioned above, the Greek word *éremos* means both loneliness and desert. The way of the prophet leads inward, away from all forms of collective community. In the desert of loneliness the ego can become the bearer of a divine being that does not stand outside us, but dwells within us. When God called the prophet Elijah, he did not speak in the wind, or in the earthquake, or in the fire, but in 'a still small voice' (1 Kings 19:11–13). When Elijah closed his eyes he heard the voice of God sounding in him.

The sibyls

A radically different method of prophesying was used by the sibyls. Where prophets were usually men, sibyls were women who had a connection with Mother Earth. They lived in remote places in Greece and Asia Minor and made unsolicited predictions of the future when in a state of ecstasy. They were highly respected, and every year thousands of people would visit their temples and caves. The first to describe their activities was the Greek philosopher Heraclitus. He wrote about them: 'The sibyl, uttering joyless things with ranting lips, not conspicuous or perfumed, yet covers more than a thousand years with her voice, thanks to the god in her.'[3]

A similar form of prophesying was practiced by the Pythia in Delphi, at the sanctuary of Apollo in Greece. She sat on a tripod over an opening in the earth, and breathed in the vapours that rose up out of this fissure and from which she received her inspirations. (Earlier authors wrote about a descent into the *adyton*, literally a place into which one may not enter.) The Pythia would utter disjointed sounds, which were then interpreted by two priests who formed them into understandable hexameters or verses. Toxicologists have recently discovered that intoxicating vapours do indeed rise up from this fissure, and that they contain ethylene, which may have caused the ecstasy observed in the Pythia. In antiquity its effect must have been even much stronger than now.

In the heyday of the sibyls, no expedition or war was started, no new city founded, without consulting the oracle. Prophets were guided by a supersensory world, whereas the sibyls followed a subterranean world of gods and goddesses. Just as prophets rose up to the highest hierarchies, sibyls had the task of turning towards the underworld and the world of the elements. There is a sibylline grotto in Cumae, Italy, that you can still visit today.

An early medieval legend relates that the sibyl of Tibur, which today is called Tivoli, predicted the coming of Christ to Emperor Augustus. This legend was impressively rendered by the author Selma Lagerlöf in her story 'The Emperor's Vision'. She places the story not in Tibur but in Rome, where Augustus one night comes to the Capitol with his entourage. He wants to consult the sibyl on whether he may build a temple to himself on this spot.

While the sibyl is in a trance, Augustus prepares to make an offering to the old gods. But in her trance the sibyl recognises a new god. In the spirit she witnesses the birth of Jesus. Filled with the spirit of prophecy, the sibyl approaches the emperor:

With one hand she clutched his wrist, with the other she
pointed to the distant East. 'Look!' she commanded, and
the emperor raised his eyes ... He saw a lowly stable behind
a steep rock wall and in the open doorway a few shepherds

kneeling. Inside the stable he saw a young mother on her knees before a little child, who lay upon a bundle of straw on the floor. And the sibyl's big, knotty fingers pointed towards the poor babe. 'Hail, Caesar!' cried the sibyl in a burst of scornful laughter. '*There* is the god who shall be worshipped on Capitoline Hill! … Upon Capitoline Hill shall Christ – the redeemer of the world – be worshipped, but not frail mortals.' When she had said this, she strode past the terror-stricken men, walked slowly down the mountain, and disappeared. On the following day, Augustus strictly forbade the people to raise any temple to him on Capitoline Hill. In place of it he built a sanctuary to the newborn God, and called it *Ara Coeli* – Heaven's Altar.[4]

We can still find a trace of this legend on the ruins of the old Capitol where a church was built called Santa Maria de Capitolo. Tradition has it that Augustus built an *Ara Coeli* on this spot after the sibyl had predicted the birth of the Messiah to him. In a curve above the altar Augustus and Mary are pictured in a fresco. It is thought that the church was built on the foundation of the temple of the goddess Juno Moneta.

The legend of the emperor's vision illustrates the prophecy of Daniel who foresaw the 'desolating sacrilege': a time when mortal men would take possession of the Holy of Holies and proclaim themselves to be God. Augustus was known for having temples dedicated to him in countless cities across the empire.[5]

Tradition also records that the sibyl of Delphi gave the last message of all sibyls to the emperor Julian the Apostate: 'This is the last oracle. There are no more. The whispering source has fallen silent.' The source of the sibyls' inspiration was exhausted. This was around the year AD 350. At that time the old clairvoyance had died out and Greek philosophy was flourishing. Thus the demise of an old clairvoyant culture coincided with the rise of a new culture of thought.

However, from early Christendom to the Renaissance the sibyls have had a place in Christianity. They are even mentioned in the Latin text of the Requiem Mass: '*Dies irae, dies illa, solvet saeclum, teste David cum Sibylla*', which translates as: 'Day of wrath, day of anger, will dissolve the world in ashes, as foretold by David and the Sibyl.'

Figures 3.1a and 3.1b: The sibyls of Delphi and Cumae as painted by Michaelangelo in the Sistine Chapel in Rome.

Figures 3.2a and 3.2b: The prophets Isaiah and Jeremiah as painted by Michaelangelo in the Sistine Chapel in Rome.

Michelangelo painted prophets and sibyls beside each other in the Sistine Chapel in Rome as though they might be brothers and sisters. Seven male prophets alternate with five female sibyls. Alongside the four so-called great prophets Isaiah, Jeremiah, Ezekiel and Daniel, the often-quoted minor prophets Joel, Zachariah and Jonah are pictured. The five sibyls shown by Michelangelo are said to have predicted the coming of the Messiah. For instance, in his Fourth Eclogue, Virgil wrote about the sibyl of Cumae that 'a new progeny of heaven will bring back the Golden Age'.

Rudolf Steiner made an interesting comparison between the sources of inspiration of the prophets and the sibyls in his lecture of December 29, 1913. In the light of the frescoes of Michelangelo he showed how the prophets are absorbed in thought in the higher spiritual world, whereas the sibyls are inspired by beings that work in nature, in the elements and in the earth. And although the clairvoyance of the sibyls belonged to a declining world that ceased to exist with the rise of autonomous thinking, in the work of the 'pagan apostle', Paul, lived an element in which the connection with spiritual beings in nature, the elements and the earth was christened.[6] In another lecture, however, he showed that sibylline forms of predicting the future are still to a certain extent justified, when he spoke of 'naïve clairvoyance' through which the return of Christ can be recognised in our time. We could call the character of Theodora, a woman who predicts the future like a modern Pythia in Steiner's mystery dramas, a Christian sibyl.[7]

Shamanism

Although atavistic clairvoyance began to disappear with the advent of autonomous thinking and the rise of Christianity, certain pre-Christian cultures and traditions persist. This brings us to shamanism, whose origins lie in Siberia and Central Asia. Shamanism is not a religion or a philosophy but a way of inducing trance states that allow the shaman to leave their body and enter the spiritual world. The more deeply a person is incarnated, however, the more radical the techniques have to become to achieve this.

During the sixth and seventh centuries, when the last forms of the Mithras religion were being practised, draconian methods were required to initiate a person. The aspirant had to suffer hunger and thirst, and for two days he was constantly beaten. From time to time he was submerged in ice-cold water. These were all methods to drive the soul and spirit out of the body – until one day the old initiation came to an end. The principle of initiation did not work anymore. What was then left was expressed by author August Strindberg in the words: 'When the gods grow old, they become demons.' When the time of the gods is past, the religion becomes decadent. Instead of gods, demons appear. This holds true for the Western world. Shamanism is still practised in some cultures today, such as by the indigenous tribes of Papua New Guinea. Anthropologists describe how their knowledge and understanding of nature is completely different from that of modern science. Their 'biology', for example, consists of a differentiated knowledge of nature spirits. To preserve this original condition, however, these tribes often have to close themselves off from the outside world.

The shamans who live in these isolated cultures often have the biggest problems with Westerners who adopt elements of the shamanic tradition and offer them in return for payment. For real shamans this is a form of desecration and shows a lack of respect for their culture. It could be considered cultural appropriation or cultural exploitation, which are forms of cultural colonialism.

One of the most flagrant examples of cultural exploitation is shown in the documentary *Enlighten Us: The Rise and Fall of James Arthur Ray*, about a man who became famous and then notorious in New Age circles. He picked up methods of Indigenous American shamans and had participants in his 'Wishing Quest' pay $10,000 per session for a retreat in which he took them into the desert of Arizona. Each of them was left alone. If they wanted to be warm, they had to pay $250 more for a Peruvian poncho. For 36 hours the participants received no food or drink. Ray not only made money with these initiation methods, he also abused them. The result was that after an hours-long session in a sweat lodge two participants died, and that others came back from this session with burns and breathing problems. The Indigenous Americans consider such practices as cultural theft and black magic. What is supposed to bring 'relief' is corrupted.

As Westerners with a history of ever-growing independence stretching behind us for centuries, we need other methods to cultivate a new connection with the spiritual world. For Carl Jung it was self-evident that in the first instance we have to make use of the archetypes of our own culture. For Jung this was not theoretical but a reality of which he had direct experience. During a journey to India, in which he deeply immersed himself in Hinduism and Buddhism, he had a dream about the Holy Grail:

> Imperiously, the dream wiped away all the intense impressions of India and swept me back to the Occident, which had formerly been expressed in the quest for the Holy Grail as well as in the search for the philosopher's stone. I was taken out of the world of India, and reminded that India was not my task, but only a part of the way – admittedly a significant one – which should carry me closer to my goal. It was as though the dream were asking me, 'What are you doing in India? Rather seek for yourself and your fellows the healing vessel, the *servator mundi*, which you urgently need. For your state is perilous; you are all in imminent danger of destroying all that centuries have built up.'[8]

This is not to say that we should turn away from other cultures. On the contrary, Jung had a genius for becoming familiar with other cultures and peoples. But if you want to follow paths of spiritual development outside of your own cultural heritage, you will eventually cut yourself off from your roots.

4

The Little Apocalypse

The heavens and the earth will pass away,
but my words will not pass away.

Luke 21:33

Shortly before his death, Christ gathers his followers together and warns them of the persecution and suffering they will face before the appearance of the Son of Man and the coming of the Kingdom of God. This discourse, known as the Little Apocalypse, appears in the Gospels of Matthew, Mark and Luke. These are often called the Synoptic Gospels, from the Greek *synopsis* meaning to 'see together', and they share comparable views of this event. The Little Apocalypse occupies a unique position between the pre-Christian forms of prophecy and the prophecies that come after Christ. It is the turning point between old and new forms of prophecy.

In pre-Christian forms of prophecy, the future prophet had to subject his ego, his 'I', to the fire trial in order to become a witness to coming events. He had to learn to speak with new tongues. The prophet was then able to express, not personally but supra-personally, what the spiritual world wanted to proclaim. A prophet would never say, 'I proclaim,' rather the spiritual world spoke through him.

Something similar took place in sibylline prophecy, albeit the source of inspiration was not in the heights but in the depths. The sibyl had to go out of herself to receive her revelations, and she achieved this through a state of ecstasy. The Greek word *ekstasis* literally means 'standing outside oneself' – excarnation.

These are two characteristic forms of prophecy, but in all forms of pre-Christian prophecy the I of the individual was absent, it played no part. With the coming of Christ, however, everything changed. The I was born. The candidate for initiation was now no longer like wax to be moulded by the hands of the hierophant; the headstrong ego started to resist. As a result, the old forms of initiation ceased to work and the mysteries fell into decadence.

But the ego has a Janus head; it is able to develop in different ways. We are all familiar with the kind of egoistic behaviour in which the I asserts itself over another, shutting them out and excluding them. Where I am, the other cannot be. The I is a king in its own realm. But the I also has the potential to become the bearer of the higher I, of standing up untouchable amid obstacles and trials (see also Chapter 6).

This is what lies behind the legend of St Christopher, the patron saint of travellers, who carries the Christ child on his shoulders across the river, only to feel the weight of the world suddenly bearing down on him. But still he remains standing against the powerful currents that threaten to sweep him away. The name Christopher, from the Greek *Christophorous*, means Christ bearer. The I of every human being is destined to become a *Christophorus*, a bearer of Christ.

The Little Apocalypse begins with a description of those who want to drive the Christ out with their ego. Matthew writes:

> As Jesus was sitting on the Mount of Olives, the disciples came to him privately. 'Tell us,' they said, 'when will this happen, and what will be the sign of your coming and of the end of the age?' Jesus answered: 'Watch out that no one deceives you. For many will come in my name, claiming, "I am the Messiah," and will deceive many.' (Matt. 24:3–5)

In this passage, Matthew uses the strongest and most complete form of 'I am' in the Greek language: *Ego eimi ho Christos* – I am the Christ (or Messiah). Usually the pronoun was not used, so that in ordinary speech *'eimi'* meant 'I am'. But here the emphasis is placed on the I – Ego *eimi* – indicating a more independent being. This happened at a time when the Caesars were worshipped as gods. Emperor Augustus let himself be deified with the proclamation: 'God has sent the saviour to the people. None will be greater than he. The gospel of the birth of the god has been fulfilled.'[1] At the time when God became a human being, human beings became pseudo-gods.

The Little Apocalypse contrasts this with the I that fulfils its true task and is able to remain standing upright throughout life's many trials. In Luke's Gospel the Little Apocalypse ends with the words of Christ:

> Be careful, or your hearts will be weighed down with
> carousing, drunkenness and the anxieties of life, and that day
> will close on you suddenly like a trap. For it will come on all
> those who live on the face of the whole earth. Be always on
> the watch, and pray that you may be able to escape all that is
> about to happen, and that you may be able to stand before the
> Son of Man. (Luke 21:34–36)

What prevents us from standing upright? 'Be careful, or your hearts will be *bareō* [Greek for heavy, weighed down] with carousing.' Drunkenness is one way of losing our footing (quite literally), the other is by allowing our hearts to be so completely weighed down by the worries of daily life (*biotikais*) that we are unable to hear what the spiritual world wants to tell us. These are the two temptations that prevent us from being able to stand upright before the Christ, both of which eventually lead to the loss of the I.

After this comes the call: 'Be always on the watch.' In Mark this call occurs in three different sentences: 'Be on guard! Be alert! Keep watch!' (Mark 13:33 and 13:37).

What is humanity's task in relation to the Second Coming? It is to be able to stand before the Son of Man. We must ask ourselves, if we are to ever stand face to face with Christ, will our I be capable of remaining upright? Will our I be then so strengthened in itself that it will be able to bear the Christ within it, just as St Christopher was able to bear the burden of the world and remain standing in the powerful currents of life?

In the Book of Revelation, Christ says in the letter to Philadelphia: 'The one who is victorious I will make a pillar in the temple of my God' (Rev. 3:12). That is the imagination of the I that remains standing upright. A pillar is not made to stand just by itself. It is made to support, to help carry, the roof of an edifice. How do we learn to stand upright? How do we learn to become a pillar? By making the ego the carrier of a higher being. The I does not exist for its own benefit, but is there to serve others. The conclusion of the Little Apocalypse demonstrates that the goal of the creation is the free human being who is able to stand face to face with Christ.

In Matthew and Luke, the Little Apocalypse takes place on the Mount of Olives, where Christ was sitting with his disciples. According to Luke: 'Each day Jesus was teaching at the temple, and each evening he went out to spend the night on the hill called the Mount of Olives' (Luke 21:37). From the Mount of Olives, which stands to the east of Jerusalem, he saw the temple in the light of the setting sun:

> Some of his disciples were remarking about how the temple
> was adorned with beautiful stones and with gifts dedicated to
> God. But Jesus said, 'As for what you see here, the time will
> come when not one stone will be left on another; every one of
> them will be thrown down.'

The temple was a colossal edifice and for the Jews it represented the ultimate solidity. In early Christendom the Temple of Solomon was considered one of the seven wonders of the world.[2] The disciples then ask Christ when these things will happen and what signs will precede them. After warning them about people who will attempt to deceive them in his name, Christ says:

When you hear of wars and uprisings, do not be frightened. These things must happen first, but the end will not come right away. (Luke 21:5–9)

This expression occurs more often with future events, both in the Little and in the Great Apocalypse: 'These things must happen.' Here, Christ is indicating that what he is prophesying is not yet the ultimate downfall of this world, nor the revelation of a new heaven and a new earth. The ultimate goal (Greek: *telos*) has not yet been reached. For this reason, the Little Apocalypse should not be confused with the Great Apocalypse, the Apocalypse of St John, which describes the beginning of a new creation – a new heaven and a new earth. Christ's prediction concerning the destruction of the temple was fulfilled seventy years later when the Romans laid siege to Jerusalem. But it is as if, in the light of the setting sun, Christ not only saw the coming events in Jerusalem, but through them those that would occur in successive ages of time. Behind the downfall of the temple he recognised the downfall of an old world.

It is worth noting that the questions asked by the disciples – when will it happen, where and how – are not clearly answered. The disciples ask: what is the *Kairos*, the moment when it will take place? (In Greek, *Kairos* expresses the critical, decisive moment.) The point here is not the downfall of the temple, but the events that follow it in which the whole creation is brought into turmoil. Then Christ says something remarkable: 'But about that day or hour no one knows, not even the angels in heaven, nor the Son, but only the Father' (Matt. 24:36). Even for Christ the decisive moment is hidden. Luke describes what will then happen:

Then he said to them: 'Nation will rise against nation, and kingdom against kingdom. There will be great earthquakes, famines and pestilences in various places, and fearful events and great signs from heaven. But before all this, they will seize you and persecute you. They will hand you over to synagogues and put you in prison, and you will be brought before kings and governors, and all on account of my name. And so you will bear testimony to me. But make up your mind not to worry beforehand how you will defend yourselves. For I will give you words and wisdom that none of your adversaries will be able to resist or contradict. You will be betrayed even by parents, brothers and sisters, relatives and friends, and they will put some of you to death. Everyone will hate you because of me. But not a hair of your head will perish. Stand firm, and you will win life.' (Luke 21:10–19)

How is that possible? Christ says that 'not a hair of your head will perish', and yet his followers will be hated, imprisoned, betrayed and even killed. But he tells them that if they stand firm, they 'will win life'. Even if a person is physically persecuted, tortured and killed, with the help of Christ the soul can overcome all trials unhurt.

Christ also describes what we now call the war of all against all: 'Nation will rise against nation, and kingdom against kingdom.' False prophets will rise and all spiritual order will be denied. Christ here uses the word *anomia*, lawlessness. And yet, as he tells us in Matthew's Gospel that 'these are the beginning of birth pains' (Matt. 24:8). Destruction has to come, but all the turmoil and suffering it brings are the birth pangs of another reality: the fall of the old world is but the beginning of what must be born from the crisis. This is the essence of apocalyptic consciousness: catastrophes are 'only' the accompanying signs of the Second Coming in which Christ reveals himself; they are the shadows of a great light. Here, Matthew invokes the imagery used by the prophet Daniel when he refers to 'the abomination that causes desolation' (Matt. 24:15 and Dan.12:11), but we have already heard from Christ that 'such things must happen' (Matt. 24:6).

Christ indicates that a time will come when Christendom will appear lost, and the only thing that will then help is *hupomonē*, patience or firmness of resolve: 'Stand firm, and you will win life'

(Matt. 24:19). The Greek word literally means 'remain under it', like a yoke you take on your shoulders, and which you keep carrying under all circumstances. There is a German proverb which translated means 'patience devours the devil'. The only thing capable of overcoming the devil is patience, for the devil has no patience. In the Book of Revelation it is said of him: 'He is filled with fury, because he knows that his time is short' (Rev.12:12).

The next part of the Little Apocalypse describes how the chaos spreads over the whole creation, even the cosmos is affected:

There will be signs in the sun, moon and stars. On the earth, nations will be in anguish and perplexity at the roaring and tossing of the sea. People will faint from terror, apprehensive of what is coming on the world, for the heavenly bodies will be shaken. At that time they will see the Son of Man coming in a cloud with power and great glory. When these things begin to take place, stand up and lift up your heads, because your redemption is drawing near. (Luke 21:25–28)

An indication of the I that has to stand upright. Everything falls into turmoil. Chaos spreads over the world of the elements and into heaven (Greek: *dynameis tōn ouranōn*), and brings oppression among the peoples. The Greek word for oppression used here is *aporia*. We are familiar with the word 'pores', which refers to the little openings in our skin. The word *a-poria* means 'without openings'. But all this is no more than the shadow cast by a great light, for then we are told people 'will see the Son of Man coming in a cloud with power and great glory'. The image of the cloud is a reference to the sphere of life, known in anthroposophy as the etheric realm. The Greek text also refers to the spiritual hierarchies. The Son of Man comes in a cloud with *dynameōs kai doxēs*, meaning the hierarchy of the Dynamis, or Virtues, who bring revelation (*doxa*). These beings are the Spirits of Movement who cause the turmoil seen in heaven and on earth.

Then the disciples ask by what sign will they be able to recognise the Son of Man, and again they are left in uncertainty. Matthew writes: 'For as lightning that comes from the east is visible even in the west, so will be the coming of the Son of Man' (Matt. 24:27). There is no indication of time nor any indication of place, only signs that we must learn to understand.

The first question the disciples asked Christ already contains the key word that will help the attentive reader understand the Little Apocalypse. After Christ predicted the downfall of the temple, they asked: 'What is the sign of your coming?' The Greek word usually translated as 'coming' or 'future' is *parousia*, but it has different meaning. It consists of the words *ousia*, 'being', and *para*, 'with' – 'being with'. You could translate it as 'abiding presence'. It is the fulfilment of the promise Christ gave at his resurrection: 'I am with you always, to the very end of the age' (Matt. 28:20).

In the Latin version of the Little Apocalypse the *parousia* was translated as *praesentia* or as *adventus*, meaning arrival. Luther translated it as 'the future of the Lord'. But it is no future, it is here and now. It is an intangible presence that can be felt by all people everywhere, just as the lightning flashes up in the east and is visible in the west.

In the diaries of the author Franz Kafka there is an empty page with just two words: *'Christus – Augenblick'*, or 'Christ – moment'. That could be as good a description as any of Christ's *parousia*. He is there one moment, then withdraws from our sight the next. To experience his *parousia* we must cultivate a spiritual presence of mind.

Maybe that is what Christ means with his call at the end of the Little Apocalypse:

Be always on the watch, and pray that you may be able to
escape all that is about to happen, and that you may be able to
stand before the Son of Man. (Luke 21:36)

The Little Apocalypse wants to make us familiar with a reality in which the future of the Second Coming is present. During his life on earth, Christ expressed this with the contradictory words: 'A time is coming and has now come' (John 4:23 and 16:32). That which is impossible in the physical world is possible in the realm of providence. The Latin word *providentia* not only means to 'foresee', but also to 'make provision' for something. Foreseeing the future and at the same time making provision for it in the here and now.

Concurrently with the presence of Christ there appears the shadow cast by the approaching light. In his second letter to the Thessalonians, Paul uses the same word *parousia* for the coming of the Antichrist. The Second Coming of Christ is preceded by the coming of the human being of lawlessness (Greek: *ho anthrōpos tēs anomias*). But that is not yet 'the day of the Lord', the Last Judgment:

> Don't let anyone deceive you in any way, for that day will not
> come until the rebellion occurs and the man of lawlessness
> is revealed, the man doomed to destruction. He will oppose
> and will exalt himself over everything that is called God or
> is worshiped, so that he sets himself up in God's temple,
> proclaiming himself to be God. Don't you remember that
> when I was with you I used to tell you these things? And
> now you know what is holding him back, so that he may be
> revealed at the proper time. (2 Thess. 2:3–6)

Who is the one who determines the decisive moment when the opposing power intervenes? In the foreground of the spectacle we see the temple that is destroyed, the world that falls into chaos. Behind it works the power of the adversary:

> The coming of the lawless one will be in accordance with
> how Satan works. He will use all sorts of displays of power
> through signs and wonders that serve the lie, and all the ways

that wickedness deceives those who are perishing. They perish because they refused to love the truth and so be saved. For this reason, God sends them a powerful delusion so that they will believe the lie and so that all will be condemned who have not believed the truth but have delighted in wickedness. (2Thess. 2:9–12)

The one who determines the decisive moment, therefore, is not the adversary, but God himself. We usually associate disastrous events with the word 'apocalypse', but the Book of Revelation begins with the words: *Apocalypsis Jesou Christou* – the Revelation of Jesus Christ. He is the one who bears and orders the life of the world. When the time has come we will see that he has the whole world in his hand.

To learn how to read the pictures of the Little and the Great Apocalypse, it is a good idea to go back to the original Greek text time and again. Most of our translations are deficient because in the Greek language the words usually have more than one meaning; they are also the expression of a totally different culture and way of thinking. The Apocalypse does not contain abstract concepts or theology, but signs: 'There will be signs in the sun, moon and stars...' But what are signs (Greek: *sēmeia*)? And what is 'the sign of the Son of Man?' (Matt. 24:30) Signs are things you have to learn to understand, like runes, the meaning of which must first be deciphered.

The language of the Little and the Great Apocalypse offers the possibility of understanding the signs of the time. But it is a risky undertaking to make connections between the signs of the Little and the Great Apocalypse and the events of our time. In our materialistic age we tend to interpret these signs literally. In the Gospel of Mark, for example, Christ proclaims that before the Second Coming can become reality 'the gospel must first be preached to all nations' (Mark 13:10). This leads some Christian sects to print the Bible in all languages and use it aggressively in their missions in the belief that they are fulfilling this commandment.

But the imagery of the Apocalypse is not physical but imaginative. There have been countless times in history, beginning with the Emperor Nero, when the Antichrist has been seen in despots. And the same is still happening today. According to fundamentalists of the Messiah Movement in The Netherlands, the newest version of the Antichrist is the World Economic Forum. On the website of this group we can read under the title 'Meeting of the Great Reset':

> It is a godless world government (the spirit of the Antichrist) and there is not one among them who believes in anything, except in world government, socialism, and communism. They still had to get one person out of the way before they could really make progress, and that was President Trump.

In countless forms of conspiracy thinking we see this phenomenon: what was originally given in the language of imaginations is attributed to groups and persons who are made scapegoats. But apocalyptic imagery is meant to be understood imaginatively, not in a purely physical sense. It refers to spiritual powers that we must learn to know and recognise. In the terminology of the Apocalypse these powers are known as the Beast (Rev. 13).

We need insight into these powers, also known as Lucifer and Ahriman, and how they work in the world. But we will only be able to develop this when we are willing to recognise how they also work in ourselves. When we carry out our daily review we might ask ourselves, 'Where was Lucifer in my life today? Where was Ahriman?' If we do that consistently we soon realise that the adversarial powers are at work just as much in us as they are in the scapegoats of our time.

A positive way to learn how to think and view things apocalyptically is to consider Rudolf Steiner's characterisation of anthroposophy as the ability to see seed or germ conditions everywhere, meaning that we can learn to look past the chaos and destruction that surrounds us to what wants to be born out of it.

We can even do this in our encounters with others. We can often find ourselves irritated by the characteristics of other people, but we can make the effort to see through those to what is trying to come into being through this imperfect human being, no matter how clumsily they express themselves. And of course, the same will be true of ourselves in relation to others. That is a way to put the Apocalypse into practice.

In pastoral care I constantly have to look beyond the person in front of me and live with the imagination of their angel who stands behind them. This element of seeing apocalyptically – past physical reality – is also necessary in assisting a dying person. What is it that wants to be born in this dying human being? This is always a crucial question for me whenever I prepare a funeral address. What seeds does this soul take with it into the life to come? What wants to be born out of this death?

The Little Apocalypse in the Gospel of Luke ends with the words: 'The heavens and the earth will pass away, but my words will not pass away.' We will in the future be more and more confronted with a perishable world. This holds true not only for every mortal human being, but also for the dying earth existence, for all forms of destruction we see around us.

I have so far described two steps for working with apocalyptic texts. The first is to learn to read the Apocalypse; the second is to learn to recognise the signs of the times, the *sēmeia*, with the help of apocalyptic imagery. But there is still a necessary third step. This is the call to live the Apocalypse. To work with these contents in such a way that they become an actual part of daily life. How can I realise the call: 'Be always on the watch ... that you may be able to escape all that is about to happen, and ... stand before the Son of Man'?

When we go to sleep at night we enter the realm of 'brief death' as it was traditionally called. Sleep is a brief death, death is a long sleep. Upon falling asleep I enter the spiritual world. Sleep is an opportunity to meet the Resurrected One. Am I capable of standing before him?

We can prepare for this moment through the daily review, in which we look back over the events of our day in reverse order. This provides us with an opportunity to reflect on our actions and to consider how they might have affected those around us, especially if, as Steiner recommended, we try to view our actions not as they unfolded from our own subjective point of view, but from the perspectives of others. And as I mentioned earlier, we can also look to see what part Lucifer and Ahriman played in our day too.

This practice mirrors the whole life review known to us from near-death experiences. In his book *Return from Tomorrow*, George Ritchie describes how the space in which he found himself was suddenly filled with light, a light brighter than a thousand suns. He still had the presence of mind to think: 'I am glad I don't have physical eyes at this moment. This light would destroy the retina in a tenth of a second.' Suddenly in this light appeared a being of light that spoke to him: 'Stand up. You are in the presence of the Son of God.'[3]

Here resounds the motif from the Little Apocalypse: '…to stand before the revelation of the Son of Man.' George Ritchie was once asked in an interview: 'But how did you know it was Christ and not an angel?' He answered: 'I saw a lot of angels in that near-death experience, but an angel cannot be compared with the light of Christ. This was so overwhelming. If I lived a million years, this encounter has been etched into my soul forever.'

5

The Apocalypse of St John

*There are three judgments. Others judge us, and this judgment
is false and incorrect, because they see only the outside. Or people
judge themselves and do so incorrectly because they see only their
own inwardness without taking into account the examples they give.
I alone completely know every soul. It is the Son of Man
who will judge the world.*

Gabrielle Bossis

It is a small step from the Little Apocalypse to the Great Apocalypse, the Revelation of St John. Both texts are called Apocalypse, both reveal the future, but in two different ways. This difference is not always perceived. The Greek word *apokalupsis* means revelation – something that was hidden is revealed. It is sometimes also translated as discovery – something that was covered is disclosed. But these two apocalypses offer different perspectives on future events.

The Little Apocalypse, which is described in Matthew, Mark and Luke, can be compared with the view from the foothills of a mountain: we can see far but the view is still somewhat limited. The Little Apocalypse describes events around the Second Coming and ends with a grand perspective: 'Heaven and earth will pass away, but my words will never pass away' (Matt. 24:35). The Apocalypse of St John, however, is like the panoramic view from the top of the mountain. The Greek words *pan horama* mean 'everything view, seeing everything'.

The Great Apocalypse begins with the Second Coming – 'Look,

he is coming with the clouds, and every eye will see him, even those who pierced him' (Rev. 1:7) – but ends with an image that, as we have seen, is only hinted at in the Little Apocalypse: 'Heaven and earth will pass away…' This panoramic view shows how the old world passes away and a new world, a new heaven and a new earth symbolised by the New Jerusalem, come into being.

The Great Apocalypse also describes the Last Judgment, which is often confused with the Second Coming although it is very different from it. In anthroposophy, the Second Coming is also called the appearance of Christ in the etheric realm, the spiritual world that borders our physical world. Rudolf Steiner said on many occasions that this is the most important event of our time. Beginning in the twentieth century, Christ appears in the etheric realm as the Lord of Karma, taking over the task that was performed for millennia by Moses, the initiate of the Jewish people. And whereas Moses always judged according to the law, Christ now brings the greatest possible blessing and harmony into the karma of human beings.[1] This difference in the way Christ and Moses work is indicated through the subtle use of language in the prologue to the Gospel of John. There, John the Evangelist writes: 'For the law was given through Moses; grace and truth came through Jesus Christ' (John 1:17). Although the Ten Commandments of Moses are an indisputable fact, Christ rises above them to a world of becoming where grace takes the place of law.

There is an important difference between the Little and the Great Apocalypse. In the Little Apocalypse, the evangelists Matthew and John were witnesses to what Christ said on the Mount of Olives. They wrote down what they had heard and seen. In the Great Apocalypse, Christ reveals himself through the writer. There is a subtle but important difference between the two. In Greek, the Apocalypse of St John begins, '*Apokalupsis Iesou Christou…*' or 'This is the revelation of Jesus Christ…' This is an important correction to our one-sided view of the apocalypse, which sees it as being only about doom, destruction and downfall. No, in this apocalypse, Jesus Christ reveals himself to be the alpha and the omega, the beginning and end of all creation. The ultimate form of the 'I AM', *ego eimi*, is used here: 'I AM the alpha and the omega' (Rev. 1:8). It is not the adversarial power, the agent of all that doom and destruction, that reveals itself in the first instance, but Christ himself.

Immediately after this, John writes in a form that is unusual for him: 'I, John, your brother and your companion...' (Rev. 1:9). This expression – '*Ego, Ioannes*' – is almost literally the alpha and omega of the Apocalypse. It appears several times, including in the last chapter where he writes: 'I, John, am the one who heard and saw these things' (Rev. 22:8).

In the Gospel of John, he remains more or less invisible. There he writes about himself in the third person singular, for example: 'The man who saw it has given testimony, and his testimony is true. He knows that he tells the truth...' (John 19:35). The grammatical I-form, which was new for John, indicates the remarkable difference between the pre-Christian and Christian forms of prophecy. The prophets of the Old Testament were, in a certain sense, the 'mouthpieces' of the divine world. This was dramatically pictured in the vision of Isaiah, whose mouth was touched with the fire of the spiritual world; only then was he allowed to speak. The pre-Christian prophets worked in a certain sense like mediums, the ego played no role. In the Apocalypse of St John, however, this form of prophecy is no longer working. John speaks on his own authority: 'I, John...' Again, this is not the supra-human *ego eimi* in which Christ speaks, but the human ego, which participates in the Revelation. John shows in a modest way the role of the ego in the first sentences of the Apocalypse:

The revelation from Jesus Christ, which God gave him to show his servants what must soon take place. He made it known by sending his angel to his servant John, who testifies to everything he saw – that is, the word of God and the testimony of Jesus Christ. (Rev. 1:1–2)

With these words, John gives even more insight into the modest role he plays in this Revelation. The pictures that appear to him are not yet the ultimate answer to the most distant future. In the prologue of the Apocalypse this sequence of active participants is then completed with the words: 'Blessed is the one who reads aloud the words of this prophecy, and blessed are those who hear it and take to heart what is written in it, because the time is near' (Rev. 1:3).

John is only a link in a golden chain that reaches from the Godhead to the earth. God gives this revelation to Jesus Christ who, through his angel, gives it to John, his servant. Now every human being can read this Apocalypse. Thus, this spiritual ladder reaches from the highest regions of the Trinity to earthly humanity.

A riddle emerges with the expression 'His angel'. Who is the angel of Jesus Christ? 'See, I send my angel before you,' says the Father, who gives his angel to the coming Messiah. In Gethsemane an angel strengthens Christ when no human being assists him anymore. Tradition says that this angel is John the Baptist. In traditional icons he is often shown as a winged being. Whereas in the physical world objects and living beings are separate, in the world of the spirit beings do not work side by side but in and through one another – they permeate each other. In this prologue of the Apocalypse, it becomes clear that when we as readers absorb its contents in ourselves, we can, just like the inspired revealer, become links in these worlds that permeate each other.

Anyone who has at least some familiarity with the complex imagery of the Apocalypse knows that it is unrealistic to try and explain these contents in one chapter. Here I will only describe the architecture of the Apocalypse in outline, upon which I will limit myself to a few crucial passages. Visually you might compare this architecture of the Apocalypse with the Temple of Solomon in its fourfold structure.

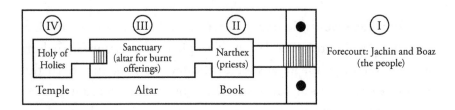

*Figure 5.1. The Temple of Solomon in its four parts (above)
is mirrored in the structure of the Apocalypse (below)*

(I)	(II)	(III)	(IV)
Physical	Astral	Lower Devachan	Upper Devachan
Seven letters	Seven seals	Seven trumpets	Seven bowls
Forecourt	Narthex: 'Book'	Sanctuary: 'Altar'	Holy of Holies: 'Temple'
(Rev. 2)	(Rev. 5)	(Rev. 8)	(Rev. 15)

Compare stages in the old initiation:

Conditions	Katharsis	Photismos	Initiation
	(Purification)	(Illumination)	(Initiation)
	Imagination	Inspiration	Intuition

In the language of the Apocalypse:

	'And I saw	'Who has ears to	'Take the book
	... and see'	hear, hear'	and eat it'

In the language of the ritual:

Gospel reading	Offertory	Transubstantiation	Communion

In the images of the Apocalypse:

Proclamation	Offering of	The earth burns	Babylon:
of the letters	the lamb	(Rev. 8)	anti-communion
(Rev. 2)	(Rev. 4)		(Rev. 17)
	The incense	The sea becomes	New Jerusalem:
	(Rev. 8)	like blood	communion
		(Rev. 21)	
		Sun, moon, and stars	
		are darkened (Rev. 8)	

One entered the temple area via the forecourt with the two columns, Jachin and Boaz. This is the place where the people gathered. The second part was the narthex where only the priests could go. The third part, the sanctuary, was where the altar for the incense offerings stood and where the incense rose. The fourth part, the hidden part, was the Holy of Holies, the *naos*. This was the actual temple part where the Godhead dwelt. In Greek there were two names for temple: *hieron*, which referred to the whole temple complex, and *naos*, the Holy of Holies.

We can recognise this fourfoldness also in the structure and composition of the Apocalypse, with the seven letters, seven seals, seven trumpets, and seven bowls of wrath (see Figure 5.1 on opposite page). We can describe the characteristics of these four parts with a few key words.

The seven letters (Rev. 1–3) may be compared with the forecourt of the temple. They have the character of an announcement, a preparation. From Chapter 5 onwards, the book with its seven seals plays an important role. The closed book can only be opened by the Lamb of God and its contents are revealed – *apocalypse* – step-by-step. In this part, the spiritual world becomes visible in images, through the spiritual faculty of imagination. After the seven seals there follows the seven trumpets, the spiritual world begins to resound; this is the stage of inspiration. In Chapter 8 the altar in heaven appears for the first time, the *naos*. Finally, in the fourth part of the Apocalypse, the seven bowls of wrath are poured out: the spiritual world becomes 'tangible' in the form of intuition. From Chapter 15 onwards the Holy of Holies appears.

We know these four stages from the process of initiation, which is described in Rudolf Steiner's book about the path of spiritual schooling *How to Know Higher Worlds*. The first part describes the conditions that prepare the candidate for initiation for the coming trials. The second part has traditionally been called purification or catharsis and is followed by a third part known as illumination.

The fourth part consists of the actual initiation. The second, third and fourth part correspond with the three stages of initiation: imagination, inspiration and intuition.

An earthly comparison may help clarify what is meant by these terms. When you look at the world through your eyes, your observation is confined, in a certain sense, to the surface of things. When the world begins to sound you penetrate more deeply into its reality than through mere observation. Finally, when you touch the world, you are, literally and figuratively, closest to it.

Thus it is also with imagination, inspiration and intuition. In imagination images of the spiritual world appear. They are more real, more colourful, more penetrating than any visual impressions; they are forever imprinted into your retina. In inspiration the spiritual world begins to sound like trumpets, and it cuts us to the marrow. Finally, in intuition we have to 'digest' the spiritual world; we take it into ourselves.

In the language of the Apocalypse these stages are presented in the following way: 'And I saw and see...' (imagination); 'He who has ears, let him hear what the spirit says to the congregations' (inspiration – the trumpets); 'Take and eat it' (intuition). In this fourth stage, an angel gives to John the quintessence of the Apocalypse in the form of a little book and tells him to eat it. It has to be digested.

We can recognise these four parts of initiation in the Apocalypse and in the imagery of the temple. They are even reflected in the structure of the Christian mass. Here, the traditional fourfoldness consists of the Gospel reading, the Offertory, the Transubstantiation and the Communion. The proclamation of the seven letters is the Gospel reading; the offering of the Lamb and the rising incense refer to the offertory; the chapter where the earth burns, the sea becomes like blood, and the sun, moon and stars change are images of the transubstantiation; and the appearance of the New Jerusalem symbolises communion.

St Augustine, in describing the history of Christianity, said that it took its course between the persecutions of the adversarial powers and the consolations of God. We can trace this alternation throughout the Apocalypse where, time and again, passages describing persecutions by the adversarial powers alternate with those describing the consolations provided by God.

In the part of the Apocalypse that is most problematic for us catastrophic events take place. In the original Greek, the word *katastrophē* means 'decisive turn' or 'turning point'. Not just for single individuals but also collectively, these catastrophes are necessary: humanity as a whole is going through the eye of the needle. This is why in his book *Christianity as Mystical Fact*, Rudolf Steiner calls the Apocalypse an 'initiation of all of humanity'.[2]

When Willem Zeylmans van Emmichoven, the first secretary general of the Anthroposophical Society in The Netherlands, was asked for his view of the future, he said: 'In the short term I am a pessimist; in the long term I am an optimist.' That is a realistic view of the future. It could even be the motto of someone writing an apocalypse in our time. Look at the disasters, illnesses, wars and famines ravaging our world today. We hardly know which way to turn. No sooner is COVID-19 on the retreat than war in Ukraine breaks out, and without a doubt that won't be the end, for as the climate activist Great Thunberg has said, 'The world is on fire.'

In connection with coming events, Rudolf Steiner spoke about the culmination of evil, which stands under the sign of the Son of Man, who declares his power with the words: 'I hold the keys of death and Hades' (Rev. 1:18). The Son of Man has power over the realm of evil, and he also gives this power to individuals who connect themselves with him.

We find an indication of this in the letter to Philadelphia where Christ says: 'These are the words of him who is holy and true, who holds the key of David. What he opens no one can shut, and what he shuts no one can open' (Rev. 3:7). The one who, along with the author, goes through the trials and stands firm in the confrontation with evil receives the power of the key to the I. Rudolf Steiner called this the key of David: 'That is the ego that has found itself within itself.'[3]

In the Apocalypse we witness the battle for the I. To use a twentieth-century term, it is a battle against the 'pollution of the I'. That was what the French author Jacques Lusseyran called it in the last lecture he gave before he died: 'The pollution of the I is more urgent, more dramatic than the pollution of the earth,' Lusseyran writes, and with these words he begins his call for the salvation of the I.[4]

In *Christianity as Mystical Fact*, Steiner shows that the Apocalypse is a work that was written for our time and our future:

> However, we notice that this is not simply an initiation of the kind known in ancient times, but a new form of initiation which is to replace the old. Unlike the ancient mysteries, Christianity does not exist only for the sake of a chosen few individuals: it is addressed to all humanity, and aspires to the religion of all people. The truth of Christianity is accessible to everyone who 'has ears to hear'. The *mystai* [initiates] of the ancient world were singled out from the multitude, but the Christian trumpets sound for all who are willing to hear them. How to respond is a matter for everyone to decide. That is why the terrors in this 'initiation of all humanity' are also so enormously enhanced.[5]

The Apocalypse is the way through the culmination of evil to the *naos*, the Holy of Holies.

Earlier in this chapter, I indicated that the pictures of the Apocalypse alternate between heaven and earth, between the trials inflicted by the adversarial powers and the help of the divine world. In his book *Christianity and Reincarnation*, Rudolf Frieling explored this composition in detail. John has sometimes been called the composer among the four evangelists, and both the Gospel of John and the Apocalypse contain countless composition secrets. Drawing on Frieling's work we can create a sequence of place and action in the Apocalypse that can help to illustrate this:

Earth: Letters to the seven congregations (Rev. 1–3).
Heaven: Throne. Sanctus. Lamb. The new song (Rev. 4–5).

Earth: Four seals (Rev. 6:1–8).
Heaven: The deceased under the altar. White garments. The fifth seal (Rev. 6: 9–12).

Earth: The sixth seal. The 144,000 are sealed (Rev. 6:13–7:18).
Heaven: The assembly before the throne. The garments washed (Rev. 7:9–8:5).

Earth: The seventh seal. The seven trumpets. The two witnesses (Rev. 8–11).
Heaven: The War in Heaven (Rev. 12).

Earth: The woman in the desert. The beast (Rev. 12:13–17).
Heaven: The new song. The Son of Man. The song of Moses (Rev. 14–15).

Earth: The seven bowls of wrath. Babylon (Rev. 16–18).
Heaven: The white horseman. War with the beast (Rev. 19:1–17).

Earth: The fiery swamp. The dragon bound (Rev. 19:18–20:3).
Heaven: The first resurrection. The thousand-year realm (Rev. 20:4–6).

Earth: The thousand-year realm. Gog and Magog (Rev. 20:7–10).
Heaven and Earth: The Last Judgment. The New Jerusalem (Rev. 20:11–Rev. 22).

In the continuing drama of events between heaven and earth, heaven is gradually purified. While order is growing in heaven, and evil is being separated out from good, chaos necessarily increases on earth. Why is that necessary? On earth we are free to choose between evil and good. The consequence of this is that these two will continue to exist side by side until the so-called evil will, in a certain sense, come to dominate everything. But human beings will remain free to make their own choices under all circumstances – albeit that in the imagery of the Apocalypse the drama of this freedom of choice becomes progressively more radical. John repeatedly describes the obstinacy of the people who turn away from the divine world. When the seven trumpets sound and the bowls of wrath are poured out, countless plagues in the form of demonic beings are set loose to sow death and destruction. And yet again and again we read that they 'did not repent of the work of their hands; they did not stop worshipping demons' (Rev. 9:20).

This is the consequence of freedom.

Faced with so much injustice, lies and demonic activity in the world, we often feel powerless and wonder why God allows it all. Why does he not intervene to create a better world? Why is it all so terribly complicated? In the lecture cycle *The Inner Experiences of Evolution*, Rudolf Steiner said something noteworthy about this all-too-human tendency to want to sit on the throne of God and tell him how to do things:

> Human beings may think, in their weakness, that the world could have been made simpler, but the gods knew better, and, therefore, did not leave the creation of the world up to human beings ... Just as three corners belong to a triangle, so to freedom belongs the possibility of evil brought about through resignation on the part of spiritual beings.[6]

If there were no evil there would be no freedom; these two are inextricably connected. It is interesting to note that in the above passage

Rudolf Steiner speaks of the renunciation of the spiritual world. We encountered this idea in Chapter 1 when the concept of *tzimtzum* was mentioned. God takes a step back to give humanity room. The psalmist formulated this radical step as follows: 'The highest heavens belong to the Lord, but the earth he has given to mankind' (Ps. 115:16). God leaves us free. He steps back to make human freedom possible – with all the risks and dangers that entails.

We also see this in the life of Christ. In his farewell address to the disciples, he says: '…it is for your good that I am going away. Unless I go away, the Advocate will not come to you; but if I go, I will send him to you' (John 16:7). Christ withdrew at his ascension to allow his disciples to be independent. The one who will then assist them after his leaving, the Holy Spirit, no longer works as an authority from outside or from above, but as a counsellor and helper from inside. Rudolf Steiner once described this in a dramatic way. According to him, if Christ had not withdrawn then his disciples would have been possessed. Christ's presence would have been so overwhelming that it would have threatened their freedom. Such renunciation grants us room to develop our own wisdom. It makes space for the ego, but also for evil, and ultimately for the loneliness that is necessary to become ourselves.

This brings us to the heart of the Apocalypse where in cryptic language the birth of the I is described. Before the war of Michael and his angels against the dragon, a great sign appears in the heavens:

A great sign appeared in heaven: a woman clothed with the sun, with the moon under her feet and a crown of twelve stars on her head. She was pregnant and cried out in pain as she was about to give birth. Then another sign appeared in heaven: an enormous red dragon with seven heads and ten horns and seven crowns on its heads. Its tail swept a third of the stars out of the sky and flung them to the earth. The dragon stood in front of the woman who was about to give birth, so that it might devour her child the moment he was born. She gave birth to a son, a male child, who 'will rule all the nations with an iron sceptre'. And her child was snatched up to God and to his throne. (Rev. 12:1–5)

John beholds the imagination of the human soul in its purest state: thoughts in the imagination of the stars, feelings in the imagination of the sun, and the will in the imagination of the moon. This moon was at all times pictured as a sickle, a crescent. Our will is in reality not like an arrow on a bow, which we aim at our target, but like the sickle of the moon that receives the light of the sun as in a bowl. This is the primal picture of the human soul.

This human soul now gives birth to 'a son, a male child'. It is completely superfluous to say that a son is a male child, but the author of the Apocalypse wants to emphasise that there is a different quality that is born here in the human being: the quality of the I. The I is a newborn child, the most future part of the human being. It is for the I that the battle of the Apocalypse is waged: 'And her child was snatched up to God and to His throne.'

Since this birth, the human being consists of two I's. What we have here on earth is but a reflection of our true, higher I, which is in the spiritual world. Rudolf Steiner once wrote: 'Let your work be the shadow that your I casts when it is shone upon by the flame of your higher self.'[7] In this sentence, the complicated relation between our work and the two I's – our earthly self and our higher self – is shown in the image of the I between the visible reality on earth and the invisible spiritual flame of our true, higher I. Long ago, the human being was in a different situation: before the Mystery of Golgotha these two were one, but, according to Rudolf Steiner, following that event the higher and the lower I were separated from each other. Human beings were thrown back onto themselves. This is expressed in the Apocalypse with the words: 'The woman fled into the wilderness to a place prepared for her by God...' (Rev. 12:6).

Paul indicated the mystery of the I in his letter to the Colossians when he wrote:

For you died, and your life is now hidden with Christ in God. When Christ, who is your life, appears, then you also will appear with him in glory. (Col. 3:3–4)

In a course for the priests of The Christian Community, Rudolf Steiner gave the following rendering of this cryptic text:

You have died, and your I has been separated from you and united with Christ in the spiritual world. However, when Christ, who bears your I, appears Himself you will also reveal yourselves with Him.[8]

The Second Coming of Christ shall in due course create the possibility for the higher I, the child, to unite itself with the human soul, the woman in the desert. In a painting from the early Middle Ages, all the elements of this mythical story are brought together (see Figure 5.2 on the next page).

High on the left we see the woman surrounded by the stars, the sun and the moon, standing before the dragon. High on the right is the child guarded by two angels and standing before the throne of God. In the centre of the painting is depicted the war in heaven:

Then war broke out in heaven. Michael and his angels fought against the dragon, and the dragon and his angels fought back. But he was not strong enough, and they lost their place in heaven. (Rev. 12:7–8)

After the war in heaven we find the woman in the desert, a symbol of loneliness (the Greek word *eremos* used here means both desert and loneliness). The woman is pictured again, in the middle on the left, only now no longer in colour like before, but as a black Madonna with wings. When she is persecuted by the serpent, which is called the Devil and Satan (the two adversarial), we are told:

Figure 5.2: Images from Chapter 12 of the Apocalypse in the
Facundus Codex, National Library, Madrid, Spain.

The woman was given the two wings of a great eagle, so that she might fly to the place prepared for her in the wilderness, where she would be taken care of for a time, times and half a time, out of the serpent's reach. (Rev. 12:14)

One cycle of time, two cycles and half a cycle: this is a classic indication of initiation. Three and a half days was the time initiation took in antiquity. The critical question for our apocalyptic age is: how does the soul get wings again? How can the soul, thrown back onto itself in loneliness, grow wings to connect with the spiritual world? Picasso once described this task, in which we let ourselves be led by higher objectives, with the following words:

All ways are open, and what will be found is unknown. It is a risky venture, a holy adventure. The uncertainty of such ventures can only be undertaken by those who know themselves secure in insecurity, who get into uncertainty and feel no guidance, who surrender in the dark to an invisible star, and let themselves be led by higher objectives instead of setting their goal within the limitations and boundaries of being human. This openness to every new insight, to every new experience, both outer and inner – that is the essential nature of modern human beings who, in all their fear of letting go, still experience the blessing of the revelation of new possibilities.[9]

In the language of the twentieth century, Picasso expressed what is portrayed in the primal picture of the woman in the desert: finding security in insecurity.

After this, the core of the Apocalypse, all hell really does break loose. The battle has been fought and heaven has been purified, but on earth the trouble is only starting. Where is Michael at this point? He seemingly leaves humanity to its own devices and pulls back. Evil then culminates in the two figures of the beast, which rise out of the sea and the earth. Then John writes: 'It [the beast] was given power to wage war against God's holy people and to conquer them' (Rev. 13:7). The 'holy people' (*hagioi*), the saints, are defeated by the beast.

Chapter 13 is one of the most difficult and depressing chapters of the Apocalypse. It shows a future in which Christianity will be a lost cause, when those who had become saints will be vanquished by the Antichrist. Here we increasingly encounter the contrary nature of the Apocalypse, which alternates between the triumph of the divine world and the triumph of the Antichrist on earth. But this chapter also contains hope; it issues a call 'for patient endurance and faithfulness on the part of God's people' (Rev. 13:10). In the previous chapter we came across the Greek word usually translated as endurance or patience: *hupomonē*, literally 'staying under it'. It is often said that patience conquers everything, and this word appears seven times in the Apocalypse. We are urged to be patient because the devil has no patience at all 'because he knows that his time is short' (Rev. 12:12).

To understand the language of the Apocalypse we need insight into the workings of the demons. We also need this in daily life to distinguish the adversarial power from Christ, for the adversarial power is able to manifest itself in the guise of Christ: Lucifer may appear in the imagination of Christ.

How is it possible to distinguish Lucifer from Christ?

Rudolf Steiner once answered this question as follows: 'Christ is pure selflessness.'[10] Everything to do with selfishness, with egoism, is part of the working of the adversarial power. Steiner also said that to be Christian is to 'look for the balance between the ahrimanic and luciferic elements'.[11] When you look for balance in your life as though you were walking on a tightrope, then, even if your balance is shaky, in that search Christ can be found.

The Apocalypse does not end with a nostalgic yearning for paradise, but with an optimistic vision of the future: the New Jerusalem. The unknown author of the Letter to the Hebrews indicates this with the words: 'For here we do not have an enduring city, but we are looking for the city that is to come' (Heb. 13:14). Anything that gives us the pleasant feeling of being at home here on earth, which we like to call our comfort zone, takes us away from true Christianity, which seeks a future when heaven and earth will enrich each other. This is the New Jerusalem, 'new' not in the sense of a subsequent chapter in a long series, but a quality that is unprecedented, unsurpassed.

The Greek language has two words for new: *kainos* and *neos*. The beginning of a new chapter is *neos*, new in the sense of the next in a series. When something is unprecedented, totally new, it is *kainos*. This is the word that is used for the New Jerusalem, where the alchemical wedding of heaven and earth takes place.

When faced with the strange language and images of the Apocalypse it might seem easy to dismiss them as the product of a much earlier culture that has since passed away, or else to believe (or hope) that what it contains relates to a future remote from our own. But we should not doubt that we live in apocalyptic times. In our own time, and in the last two centuries, apocalyptic fragments have come to light under exceptional circumstances.

In his book *Dichter erzählen ihre Träume* (Poets Tell Their Dreams), Martin Kiessig gathers an interesting collection of dreams of artists from across two centuries, including many examples of twentieth-century apocalypses. Well before the Second World War broke out, dreams and visions appeared foreshadowing coming events. The poet Emil Barth describes an 'apocalyptic vision' that he had during the night of June 13, 1938:

> I saw a gigantic part of the earth floating in the dusk of the
> downfall, like a block of ice floating in water, the edges of
> which were crumbling – a slowly sinking continent that had
> the contours of Europe. The dark flood washed over the land
> while the water was constantly rising, a handbreadth, a foot, a
> yard high. The night became more and more shoreless under a
> heaven torn by clouds. The whole cosmic space was filled with the

desperate cries of countless drowning, struggling people. At the same time in an irrevocable diagonal, endless columns of troops were marching on this sinking continent, splashing through the water, moved and permeated by a terrible discipline ... They emerged as from the depth of the night, row after row, unmoved by the chaos and despair around – stamping their march through the black flood. Then out of the boundless wilderness of space and water approached a floating, shadowy hulk, something like an icebreaker, with gigantic violence. A thrust shakes the continent and splits and tears the land into pieces. And while the shadow of fate pushed into the gap without a sound, the broken continent raised itself high out of the water with all the teeming life and sank in a few moments as a wreck into the black, silent abyss.[12]

In pastoral care I encounter apocalyptic motifs from time to time. Shortly before falling asleep the person who dreamt the following images had an impressive experience of an approaching thunderstorm: clouds stacking up in the sky and rolling in slowly, becoming dark and eventually discharging themselves in lightning and thunder. During the night, this person saw in a clear dream the same clouds appearing again over the city. Life there continued in its normal way, while the clouds stacked up above the city rush. Strange, grotesque forms were growing. The person wrote:

> The clouds above the city started to move in spiralling forms.
> Under them enormous figures appeared formed by the clouds,
> forms like gigantic angel beings, which now brought forth
> from these clouds something like lava that flowed over the city,
> while life in the city was simply continuing normally.

Looking back on the dream this person writes: 'I was surprised that I had no feeling of fear. It was more a feeling, a knowing, like this has to happen.'

This dream image shows some similarity with the Apocalypse, no matter how modestly: the physical world becomes transparent to spiritual reality. The writer of the Apocalypse received the imagination, inspiration and intuition of his Revelation because this is: 'The revelation from Jesus Christ, which God gave him to show his servants what must soon take place' (Rev. 1:1). It *must* take place. Thus, the person who recorded this dream had no feeling of fear, even though she was seeing the physical world becoming engulfed in spiritual fire. They represent images of a necessary downfall, which is at the same time the beginning of a resurrection.

When Anna Samweber had an imagination of the city of Berlin engulfed in a sea of fire, she asked Rudolf Steiner if he had words for the events that were coming.[13] Thereupon Rudolf Steiner wrote the verse *Den Berliner Freunden*. Its central motif is the imagination:

And the downfall of outer appearance
Shall become the rising
Of the soul's innermost being.[14]

Figure 5.3: Dream image with apocalyptic motifs.

The downfall of the outer world must lead to the rise of the soul's innermost being.

To conclude this chapter, I will mention a few possibilities to work with the reality of the Apocalypse.

Is it possible to prepare for the New Jerusalem? When someone every day or every night is in contact with a deceased loved one through a meditative connection, that person practises, in a certain sense, the alternation between heaven and earth. In my book *Ways into Western Meditation*, I dedicated a chapter to the theme of meditating for and with the deceased. How can we, in a healthy contact with the deceased, alternate between the earth and the spiritual world? The interaction with the deceased is a building stone for the New Jerusalem.

With 'a healthy contact' I mean learning to work with the key of David, which opens what no one can shut, and which shuts what no one can open (Rev. 3:7). This is a quality we continuously need in our daily life, also in our contact with the deceased. When we want to maintain healthy relationships, we must guard the threshold of our inner being. If we keep the door open day and night, we will get uninvited guests. Blind faith benefits no one, neither myself nor my visitors. Likewise, if we keep the door closed day and night, we will become estranged from everything and everyone.

Nothing is so important in our apocalyptic time as guarding the threshold. That holds true for our contact with the living and the dead, with the world that knocks on our door – literally and figuratively. Only with the key of David – the ego that has found itself within itself, according to Rudolf Steiner – are we able both to keep standing upright, and to offer help to others without losing ourselves. In the middle between blind faith and blind fear, and always with the help of the spiritual world, confidence and trust in ourselves and in the other can grow.

6

Freedom and Inevitability

Jesse Mulder

*Then he turned the medal and found to his surprise an inscription
on the back. It consisted of four short words in beautiful curly letters: 'Do
what you want.' These words, he thought, expressed permission,
no, rather an exhortation to do everything he felt like.*

The Neverending Story, Michael Ende

The previous chapters have taken us on a colourful journey through
various mythologies, prophecies and other forms of predicting the
future. We have travelled from ancient times to more recent times
ones and been given a glimpse of the future that can be found in the
Little and the Great Apocalypse of the New Testament. We have thus
obtained what we might call 'a brief history of the future', an overview
of how people were able to arrive at a view of the future of the earth.

An important element in this 'history of the future' was the demise
of the old, pre-Christian forms of predictions. The methods by which
one arrived at visions of the future in those times are, as was stated at
the end of Chapter 3, no longer tenable. Although such methods have
remained serviceable into post-Christian times in particular contexts,
we still have to conclude that the coming of Christ on earth signifies
a turning point in this regard. As was already pointed out in the
chapter on the Little Apocalypse, this has everything to do with the
development of the human I, which comes to itself by separating itself
out through *eremos*: loneliness.

Formerly, people were able to arrive at pictures of the future
because they 'turned off' their I, so to speak. This enabled them to

become a mouthpiece for that which revealed a view of the future out of invisible realms. The old, pre-Christian forms of prediction were therefore based on the ability to subdue one's own inner I activity. But around the time that Christ appeared on earth, this ability gradually ceased. We might in this connection think of the well-known event during Holy Week when Christ did not find any fruits on the fig tree. The fig tree represented a picture of the old mysteries, the old forms of predicting the future that were no longer able to bear fruit. The fig tree had withered.

The modern I no longer lets itself be pushed aside; it wants to assert itself here on earth. For that reason, old forms of ecstasy, prophecy and initiation are no longer appropriate.

Freedom and inevitability as counterpoles

Our I becomes the critical element for everything. Why is this such a crucial fact? The key to this lies in the first word in the title of this chapter: freedom. We have become independent beings who have separated themselves out from spiritual world. We are no longer mere creatures under the guardianship of the angelic hierarchies; we have become autonomous. As free entities we increasingly influence how the development of humanity and the world should proceed. We thus progress from being creatures to becoming co-creators in the great whole.

This step can be connected with the coming of Christ to the earth. We can clearly see that the stamp we humans have impressed on the earth since that time has become larger and more distinct, particularly in the past few centuries. As was pointed out in the first chapter, we can speak today of a new era in the history of the earth called the Anthropocene. Instead of naming the period after some geologic feature, the human being, the *anthrōpos*, has itself become the determining factor for the earth as a whole.

If we take this concept of freedom seriously, the whole idea of predicting the future seems impossible. How can we predict what the future will look like if human beings are free to act, instead of being compelled to follow some predetermined divine plan? When we look at it in that way, we might be surprised that it is precisely in the New Testament that we find the apocalyptic vistas described in the last two chapters. Doesn't Christ's incarnation mark the moment when the free I begins to emancipate itself? What is all this talk then about things that *must* happen? How can it be that the author of the Apocalypse can see ahead to what is going to happen on earth in the rhythm of the seven letters, the seven seals, the seven trumpets and the seven bowls of wrath? And how can it be established that there will be something as frightful as a war of all against all?

Succinctly formulated you could summarise these questions as follows. If such future things really *are* established facts, it does not matter what we do, for wherever we turn we will end up in that war anyway.

This brings us to the second word in the title of this chapter: inevitability. It would seem that where this inexorable necessity reigns, there cannot be any room for freedom: they are incompatible.

In this chapter I intend to take a step back and provide an overview of the worlds that are connected with the concepts of freedom and inevitability. In doing so it will become clear that they are not mutually exclusive. Indeed, they even depend on each other.

Karma and reincarnation: a further dimension of the problem

Before we embark on a closer exploration of freedom and inevitability, it is good to sketch another dimension of this question. On the basis of my previous comments describing the tension we can feel between freedom and inevitability, we might be tempted to conclude that this is a question of enormous importance, concerning as it does humanity and world events as a whole. It appears distant from our individual lives in the here and now.

However, this would be a misconception. As Rudolf Steiner repeatedly emphasised in his last course for Christian Community priests, we should learn to see the Apocalypse more personally and not just as a view of a future that is still remote from us. We have already seen that this is indicated in the Book of Revelation itself with the intriguing phrase, '...the time is pressing, and is already come' – a theme that will be discussed more in the next chapter. More and more we must become 'apocalyptists' ourselves.

It is helpful to realise that the question of freedom and inevitability also relates to karma and reincarnation. What happens in my life – what I experience in the way of adversity and opportunity, talents and limitations, friendships and conflicts, successes and setbacks – they don't come from nowhere. It is the *inevitable* result of my former lives on earth. Here, too, the question may arise how such karmic inevitability can go together with freedom.

For me personally, questions relating to karmic connections became particularly concrete when, around the birth of my two daughters, I started to explore the question of incarnation more intensively – the path taken by souls from pre-birth worlds to physical existence on earth.

Rudolf Steiner spoke extensively about the process a human soul goes through on the way to a new life. In the time before their next earthly birth they work to prepare a physical body that will be a suitable vehicle for the coming incarnation. This takes place across the generations, meaning that not only does such an unborn soul help their future parents to find each other, they also help their grandparents and their great-grandparents to find each other, all so that the right conditions can be prepared for their incarnation. According to Steiner:

A great, great… grandfather of yours, way back in the sixteenth
century, fell in love with a great, great… grandmother. They
felt the urge to come together, and there, in this urge, you were
already working into the earthly world from spiritual worlds.[1]

This perspective on pre-birth life is an amazing thing when you
think about it. Here I am, supposing that I myself am trying to shape
my life out of freedom, and that my wife and I made a conscious choice
to have a family together. Of course, I am living under the assumption
that it was up to us (and therefore also up to me individually) to make
that choice, and that I could also have chosen *not* to have a family. Now
I have to imagine that my children, long before I was born, were already
working on their incarnation with us as their parents! And further,
that before my own birth, I was also working so that *my* parents would
come together, not only to make my own incarnation possible, but also
those of my two daughters. And looking towards the future, in the birth
of my own daughters, unborn souls were perhaps working who will
only come to earth in later generations: my grandchildren and great-
grandchildren.

When I try to create a lively picture in my mind of all that traffic
among the unborn, with all the threads that are spun there of which we,
with our earthly consciousness, are completely unaware, then a feeling
can sneak up on me that perhaps I don't live quite so actively and freely
in my own life as I previously thought, and that instead I merely carry
out what was put in place long ago in hidden, pre-birth heights. I might
then be inclined to feel that I am just the vehicle, the instrument, for
the inevitabilities of karma. Where then is my freedom?

A simple solution?

From an individual perspective we can feel caught in a paradoxical
situation when we consider these ideas. On the one hand, we know

ourselves to be free; on the other hand, we feel our lives to be woven into a web of inevitabilities. This creates a fundamental tension between freedom and inevitability.

We might at first attempt to resolve this tension in what appears to be an obvious way. Even if *some* of the things that are coming are inevitable, not *everything* has to be. While the web of inevitability may be tightly spun, there may still be places where the threads have not yet been woven together. As long as not *everything* is inevitable, then there is at least some room for freedom.

And yet, upon closer inspection, this solution turns out to be only an apparent one. It is a solution that neatly separates freedom and inevitability and therefore avoids the true confrontation between these two concepts. According to this view, where inevitability reigns there can be no freedom. In other words, nothing we do out of freedom makes any difference to what is inevitable.

This unsatisfactory view of things becomes all the more apparent when you consider that, from the perspective of karma and reincarnation, the inevitable things are precisely the *essential* things. To be more concrete: if all the essential encounters in my life are karmically determined and therefore inevitable – including my friendships and my choice to have a family – then there is only room for freedom in the trivial things in life. I may then perhaps still have freedom in choosing the shirt I will wear today, or what ice cream flavour I choose, but not which partner I choose, what profession I choose or whether I will have a family.

But right away we feel that this is an absurd view. The development of freedom cannot be for the sole purpose of indulging our pleasure in the trivial moments of life that have no other consequences. No, our freedom *must* have to do with the essential things, and therefore with the inevitable things. But how exactly?

Negative freedom

We can take another step towards solving the problem if we try to obtain a more substantial, more encompassing concept of freedom, for freedom is not a simple concept at all.

When we think of freedom, we often think of what in modern philosophy is called 'negative freedom'.[2] Negative freedom is being free *from* something: for example, freedom from limitations and hindrances. It is called 'negative' not because it is wrong, but because the point is the *absence* of obstacles. One's negative freedom is greater the fewer obstacles there are in one's way. If I am shut up in a cell I am limited in my movements in space; when I am liberated from that cell I can stand and go where I want. If my hands are bound, I am limited in what I can do; once my shackles are removed I have my hands free and can do with them what I want. If I live in great poverty I am very limited in what I can do; when I have plenty of money I have many more possibilities.

Negative freedom is therefore about the space in which you can do what you want. There are, of course, still limitations. For instance, there is this annoying gravity, which prevents me from freely floating through the air. Or to take a more serious example, there are always people who are standing in my way, sometimes just because they are there. From the perspective of negative freedom my fellow human beings can quickly become obstacles. They have *opinions* on whatever I do, they *react* to this, and moreover they also *want* all kinds of things, not seldom something different from what I want. This leads to many collisions and hassles.

From negative to positive freedom:
The Neverending Story

Negative freedom is the space to do what you want. In the well-known book *The Neverending Story* by Michael Ende, those words appear on an amulet with two snakes biting each other's tail. Originally published in 1979, this is an extremely instructive story on the subject of freedom.

The main character, Bastiaan, is an imaginative eleven-year-old boy who is often bullied at school; at home he is neglected by his father, who is overcome with grief by the death of Bastiaan's mother. Bastiaan becomes fascinated by a mysterious book called *The Neverending Story*. It tells the story of a great empire called Fantasia that is threatened by a mysterious 'Nothing'. The whole realm is slowly disappearing into this Nothing and Bastiaan learns this is because the Little Empress is ill. He discovers that the only salvation for the empire is for the Little Empress to receive a new name, and that *he*, the reader of the book, must give her this name. Bastiaan calls her Moon Child, and no sooner has he done this than he finds himself in the realm of Fantasia. Or rather what is left of it, for only one grain of sand remains. The Little Empress gives this to him, along with the amulet inscribed with the words DO WHAT YOU WANT.

So now I can do what I feel like, thinks Bastiaan.

Driven by his own fantasy, Bastiaan creates a new Fantasia out of this one grain of sand where he once again goes from one adventure to another – all of which are products of his own wishes. As soon as something begins to bore him, a new wish rises up in him that translates itself right away into a new piece of Fantasia, a new piece of reality. This is of course the height of negative freedom! There are no limits to what Bastiaan can wish for himself. He thus becomes a brave, celebrated hero: strong, courageous, wise, the kind he always liked to imagine. He leaves behind the bothersome limitations of his existence on earth, his fears, his cowardice, his shame, his lack of endurance. Fantasia is now all about Bastiaan; the people and creatures that appear in it are mostly characters in *his* story.

This is a wonderful picture of how negative freedom functions. It creates a space in which we can indulge ourselves as independent individuals, in which we can do *at will* whatever we like. But eventually this leads to a very important question: what are we going to do in that free space? Negative freedom is called 'negative' precisely because it doesn't provide an answer to that question. Negative freedom gives us space, but no direction. The reverse of this is *positive* freedom, which is not freedom *from* limitations, but freedom to find the right way in life.

For Bastiaan, who simply follows his immediate desires and wishes, this question only slowly comes to life. This is expressed in a profound and beautiful way: with each wish that is fulfilled, Bastiaan loses a piece of his previous self, until he even forgets his own name.

But then, at the end of the story, he finds something that touches him deeply, even though he has forgotten everything else: a dream picture in which his own father appears enclosed in a block of ice. Bastiaan no longer recognises him at this point, and yet it is this picture of his isolated and imprisoned father, coupled with his own intense wish for the ice to thaw, that in the end helps Bastiaan find his way back to the human world.

It is the first time during his long adventure in Fantasia that Bastiaan's wish takes on a new character. He does not create a fantasy world in which he turns away from the reality of his life on earth, but instead makes a wish that comes out of his current life situation. It is the wish to love and to give love to another. His earlier wishes – to be handsome, strong, brave, and wise – made him forget the reality of his own existence. To be more precise, they made him forget the *inevitabilities* of his own existence. But this new wish, which takes him back to his own home, his father, and his life on earth, this new wish actually embraces these inevitabilities.

The Neverending Story can thus help us develop our concept of freedom. It leads us from negative freedom, which views inevitabilities as limitations and hindrances to be cast aside, to positive freedom, which directs itself according to these very inevitabilities. It embraces them and takes them a step further. Freedom and inevitability thus no longer exclude each other.

Inevitability as a basis for freedom

When we consider only negative freedom, inevitabilities show themselves as hindrances that restrict our freedom. When we picture positive freedom, however, these same inevitabilities become a basis for answering the question: 'What am I going to do with my freedom?', which is an altogether different situation. Inevitabilities are then no longer external matters that have nothing to do with us, rather they become matters that in their essence do indeed concern us.

So it is with Bastiaan in *The Neverending Story*. What he experiences as his own negative characteristics – his fearfulness, his shame, his lack of athleticism, his dreaminess – are at first hindrances for him. He can't help them; he is stuck with them. It is therefore an enormous increase in negative freedom for him when he can free himself from them in Fantasia. All he has to do is wish to be strong and brave and he is it right away!

Towards the end of the story, however, his relationship to those inevitabilities he first felt stuck with begins to change. He now sees them as a true part of himself and can therefore start doing something *about* them. Inevitability is not the *opposite* of freedom, but rather turns out to be the *basis* for a positive freedom. Instead of seeing obstacles and limitations as existing in opposition to our freedom, we now see freedom and inevitability as two sides of the same coin.

This is a very fruitful perspective when we're trying to reconcile ourselves to the karmic necessities, the inevitabilities of destiny, that I mentioned before. As long as we consider these as external factors that hinder us in our freedom, then we won't make much progress. Only when we begin to experience them as parts of ourselves, as the necessary basis for our search for a meaningful direction in life, can we build a relationship to them that can be helpful and satisfying.

Going back to my earlier example, this is how I also started viewing the arrival of my daughters. It's not that I wasn't free in my choice to have a family, for since my childhood I had imagined that

I would have two daughters. At this point, I suspect that my unborn daughters were already working in me to that effect, so that without realising it, I took that activity as the basis for my choice.

The resistance we initially feel when we learn of all the karmic inevitabilities woven into our lives is nothing but our annoyance at what we perceive to be restrictions on our freedom. But when we look at it from the perspective of positive freedom, we can become grateful for those very obstacles and adversities, for they point the way in our search for what positive freedom really is: a meaningful course through life.

Freedom, self-centeredness and evil

To find our way back to the more encompassing, apocalyptic images of the future that we encountered in the previous chapters, we must take one last step. *The Neverending Story* can help us again with this. As I have already indicated, Bastiaan's last wish with which he finds his way back to his own world again differs from all his other wishes in that he does not wish something for himself, but for his father.

Bastiaan's Fantasia was a very self-centred world; for the most part it was all about him (not everything, it's true, but we don't need to go into that here.) This self-centeredness is inextricably connected with negative freedom. In negative freedom every I becomes a ruler in a little world of its own, a despot who tolerates only the most essential restrictions on their freedom. Such pure, negative freedom inevitably leads to splintering and opposition among people for, as I wrote earlier, from the perspective of negative freedom the other human being can quite easily become an obstacle.

When we consider it in this way, we begin to understand why the Apocalypse describes a future war of all against all. This is not a war in which one half of humanity battles against the other half, but a war in which each individual wars against every other individual.

That is the consequence of a one-sided development of the I through negative freedom. The question we have to ask ourselves is therefore not: 'Will I stand on the right side in that war?', for there is no right side. The only question is: 'Can I avoid getting mixed up in it as little as possible?'

What is it that is at work in such a one-sided development of the I that it remains stuck at the level of negative freedom? Why does it lead to this war of all against all? We have already learned that positive freedom orients itself according to life's inevitabilities in order to find the right direction for our actions, and that orientation is lacking when the I is basking in negative freedom. But it would be an illusion to think that, just because this orientation is missing, there is no directing power at all. If we do not find direction in our lives through positive freedom, then it will be supplied by the adversarial powers. And of course, it is the adversarial powers that cause the chaos, confusion and war.

The catastrophes that are so often described in the Apocalypse are therefore hidden as seeds of evil in negative freedom. Precisely because we are free beings in development, it is necessary, inevitable even, that evil arises and manifests itself in the world. The inevitability of these apocalyptic conditions is therefore the shadow side of freedom. In this apocalyptic picture, inevitability and freedom also turn out to be two sides of the same coin.

It is interesting that even this more apocalyptic aspect of freedom can also be found in *The Neverending Story*. At first, Bastiaan interprets the instruction 'do what you want' as 'I can do whatever I feel like'. In the beginning that seems so innocent. Out of his fantasy he creates, from the one grain of sand, the remnant of old Fantasia that the Little Empress gives him, a whole new, colourful Fantasia. But over the course of the story his wishes take on an increasingly darker nature. He abandons and betrays his friends, abuses his position of power, and eventually wants to assume absolute control over 'his' Fantasia and be crowned Emperor, which leads to war and chaos. Expressed in anthroposophical terms, he descends from a culture-creating, imaginative, luciferic beginning, into an ever-darker ahrimanic abyss. Negative freedom, when completely unfettered, may be harmless in the beginning, a game in which we indulge ourselves, but it ends with destructive and warlike urges. This has been woven quite impressively into *The Neverending Story*.

Ahriman and Christ: the spiritual foundation of freedom

In one of the so-called Michael Letters, Rudolf Steiner makes a profound statement in which he succinctly summarises the spiritual dimension of human freedom.[3] He describes how human beings have developed their wide-awake I-consciousness by emancipating themselves step-by-step from the divine-spiritual world in which they were originally embedded. The result of this is that in our modern time we experience the outside world as a purely material, sense-perceptible fact: something purely external to us in which there is nothing spiritual to discover. This was the fertile soil in which our materialistic science could grow.

This seemingly 'God-forsaken' world is also the perfect environment for attaining an experience of negative freedom. We find ourselves in a physical-sensory world that does not give us any direction in how to act. We can take up the material things that surround us here on earth and use them to develop art, culture and technology. It is actually very nice to be able to be your own boss in this way, to do what you want without having to bother about the spiritual, cosmic order.

Now, in this Michael Letter, Rudolf Steiner explains that our freedom is guaranteed by the fact that in earthly life we are presented with two basic possibilities, and that these possibilities are connected with two spiritual beings. On the one hand, we might feel so good to be independent that out of our negative freedom we choose to continue in this way. In that case we unconsciously allow Ahriman to direct our lives; we make ourselves dependent on him. On the other hand, we can take on the challenge of positive freedom and find our meaningful place within the cosmic whole once again. In doing so we turn to Christ, the *Logos*, the Word of Worlds, who is our connection to the cosmos and who gives us the freedom to find the right direction.

St Paul expressed this in his famous words: 'Not I, but Christ in me' (Gal. 2:20). Why did he write it this way? He could have written, 'Not I, but Christ', but the addition of 'in me' here is essential. The I has an important role to play, and the point is not to rub it out or overcome it as occurred in pre-Christian times. We are called to find the way to Christ *through the I*. The combination of 'not I' with the addition of 'in me' is the secret of the I. 'Not I' refers in fact to the negative freedom in which only the adversarial powers are active if we don't find our orientation in life. But in Christ, in 'Christ in me', we can find the bridge to positive freedom. It is absolutely inevitable that we find this bridge to Christ, but – and here we arrive at the most perfect unity of inevitability and freedom – this is an inevitability that can be realised exclusively out of freedom. Nothing can force us to turn to Christ.

Ahriman or Christ: this is the fundamental choice facing us in our current era according to Rudolf Steiner. Besides Ahriman we also have to consider Lucifer, as well as other adversarial powers – as was indicated in earlier chapters. It is therefore important that we speak about demonology not in an abstract way but very concretely. Nevertheless, we can say that, just as *The Neverending Story* charts a path from a fantastic, luciferic phase to a power-driven ahrimanic phase, so, too, in the development of earthly humanity, Lucifer celebrated his high point in ancient, pre-Christian times, whilst Ahriman rules over our modern, scientific-technological era.[4] The culmination of the latter still lies in the distant future. It is Ahriman who is indicated in the Gospel of John as the 'master of this world', and of whom Christ says: 'Already the master of this world is coming, but he cannot touch me' (John 14:30).

Apocalyptic concluding observation

Thus we have returned to the subject of apocalyptic predictions. We have seen how the inevitability of all the chaos, confusion, war and suffering that we find in those predictions are connected with our freedom – more specifically, our freedom in its *negative* aspect. But we must not forget the other side of this coin. If the ultimate choice is between Ahriman and Christ, we must not forget that Christ says of the former: '...the prince of this world now stands condemned' (John 16:11). We already know that what Ahriman wants – to chain human beings to earthly existence, to make us materialists in our thinking, and in our actions let us indulge ourselves purely in our instincts – we know that this is doomed to fail.

But while 'heaven and earth will pass away', at the end of the Apocalypse we are shown how the New Jerusalem descends to earth from on high. Just as the rise, and even the triumph, of evil on earth is inevitable, so too is it inevitable that it will ultimately be vanquished. As we will see later in this book, it will even be transformed.

With this we can further enrich our picture of the relationship between freedom and inevitability. No matter how bleak things may become, in the end everything that happens will be taken up into the wise world order, including evil. This is a notion that can carry us through every storm, as long as we generate enough endurance and patience: *hupomonē.*

It can be fruitful for our lives if, in full consciousness of the coming chaos, we remain confident that ultimately everything will get better. That is a genuinely apocalyptic mood, and such an apocalyptic mood is justifiable in our time. We need this mood to build the right relationship to all the fierce and drastic things that can happen in the world and in our own lives. But it is not a mood that is easily acquired and maintained. If we're not careful, such insights can become banal and flat, and then rather than helping us, they become obstacles. They make us complacent, assured as we are that eventually everything will turn out fine. And with that we have put ourselves to sleep.

Or else we think that regardless of what happens, all of civilisation must first come to an end in the big war of all against all. But this way we lose the strength needed to make any sort of commitment in life. This can help us realise that the really essential truths in life cannot be taken superficially. We must grow into them if we are to absorb them inwardly in the right way. Only then can they become a powerful help in life.

In order to avoid the pitfalls created by a delusional optimism or a paralysing pessimism, it is necessary to penetrate more deeply into the inevitability of the evil that is coming, as well as the inevitability of the good that will be victorious, and to consider them both in their mutual relationship. For as we have seen, it is precisely these two inevitabilities, which we have identified with Ahriman and Christ, that form the foundation of human freedom in our time. Both are inevitable, but how deeply we will descend into the valley of evil ultimately depends on how we as human beings, both individually and collectively, relate to them.

With this in mind, we can form for ourselves in the subsequent chapters a more concrete picture of the fundamental tasks facing modern humanity.

7

The Counterstream of Time

'I wish it didn't have to happen in my time,' said Frodo. 'So do I,' said Gandalf, 'and the same goes for anyone who has to go through such times. But it is not up to them to decide that. The only thing we have to decide is what we are going to do with the time we have been given.'

J.R.R. Tolkien, *The Fellowship of the Ring*

With the chapter on freedom and inevitability we have left the old forms of predicting the future behind us. We will now focus on the present and the future. Not, of course, on predictions that are etched in stone but on tendencies, possibilities and obstacles that we can discern in society today – in brief, in 'liquid modernity'. I realise that for many, looking back on old forms of predictions may at best be of little interest, and at worst a waste of effort. But because of this review I realise more than ever what the potential, as well as the limitations and one-sidedness, of our ideas of the future are as these are proclaimed by the conventional sciences.

These days there are thousands of mediums walking around who proclaim with great certainty what will happen to us in the future. But it is mostly muddy water that flows through the channels of mediums, even though they call it 'clairvoyance'. In order to become a mouthpiece of the spiritual world the medium must first suppress or even eliminate their I, but whoever enters the spiritual world without clear consciousness and sober judgment soon falls prey to the illusions of Lucifer and Ahriman. Even in ancient Delphi it was impossible to directly understand the message of the Pythia, the prophetess. What was dragged up unconsciously from the depths through old clairvoyance had to be translated by an initiated priest. This is the essential difference between clairvoyance and initiation: the clairvoyant may be able to see, but they do not necessarily have insight into what they see.

With the decline of the old clairvoyance (known as the Twilight of the Gods in Germanic mythology) not only did old capacities disappear, but new capacities were born. In ancient Greece these appeared on the one hand in philosophy and independent thinking, and on the other as the birth of conscience.

In Aeschylus' tragedy *Orestes*, the principal character is persecuted by the Erinyes, the goddesses of vengeance, after he has killed his mother. A few decades later Euripides wrote a tragedy on the same theme. But whereas Aeschylus placed the goddesses of vengeance on the stage, Euripides, for the first time in literature, used the word 'conscience', from the Greek *sun-eidesis*, meaning, 'knowing together'. No longer does the voice of the gods sound from outside, instead conscience speaks within a person's own soul. The emergence of these two capacities, independent thinking and conscience, marks the beginning of the development of the separate, enclosed personality. To the extent that we take part in the continuing development of humanity, we cannot escape from this loss which at the same time opens new possibilities.

Another capacity also emerged, though somewhat later, due to the loss of the old clairvoyance. According to Rudolf Steiner, by the thirteenth century (he gave the year 1250) the process of emancipation from the spiritual world had progressed so far that even the great initiates were no longer able to see into the spiritual world when they were incarnated on earth.[1] As a compensation for this, a new capacity was born, the birth of which we can follow step-by-step. In medieval German the word *ahnen* appeared, meaning 'to surmise'. We are no longer clairvoyant, but there is a faculty that gives us a presentiment of the future. These are the three gifts we can develop that will form the basis for the new clairvoyance: the capacity to think, our conscience, and our ability to have presentiments of the future.

However, when we neglect these qualities and fall back on the unconscious and subconscious, we call forth destructive powers. This danger was famously depicted in an etching by the eighteenth-century artist Francisco de Goya. He drew himself asleep at his desk surrounded by an army of demonic beings, owls, bats and strange monstrosities. He called it 'The Sleep of Reason Producers Monsters'.

Hence, my plea for common sense, particularly with things like predictions, for one has to separate the wheat from the chaff.

Figure: 7.1: The Sleep of Reason Produces Monsters by
Francisco Goya (1797–99). From the series Los Caprichos.

This brings us to the theme of this chapter: the counterstream of time. We usually think about time in terms of causality, of cause and effect, with what comes before being the cause of what comes later. We have become so accustomed to this that our methodologies for prognoses are mostly based on this. Based on the situation today we draw conclusions from it for tomorrow. But history shows us that reality is usually very different. Many of us did not foresee that while we were all obsessed with the COVID-19 pandemic, a war was brewing in Ukraine. Our daily use of language has a sense for a different stream of time. We speak of foreshadowing, when the future seems to throw its shadow forward, and we say that something 'is in the air'.

In the New Testament the counterstream of time is more than once expressed in the words of Christ: 'A time is coming and in fact has come' (John 16:32). The initiate has to some extent the capacity to recognise that 'the present is pregnant with the future', as the French philosopher Diderot once said.

This concept of the counterstream of time also stands at the beginning of anthroposophy. In a personal conversation with the French writer and philosopher Eduard Schuré, Rudolf Steiner spoke of a meeting he had with an initiate when he was eighteen, around the time of his first moon node (eighteen years and seven months). He told Schuré: 'I learned from this master that there is a forward evolution and also a reverse evolution that interferes with it – the occult-astral stream of time. This is the prerequisite for spiritual beholding.' Through this encounter Steiner became aware of the counterstream of time; he realised that time not only flows forwards chronologically, but also backwards.[2]

The Greeks knew two gods of time: Chronos and Kairos. Chronos is the god who eats his own children, he is the wear and tear of time that ultimately destroys everything. Kairos is the god who comes out of the future. Of Alexander the Great it was said that he was able to seize the god Kairos by his waving hair as he flew by. That was the hallmark of a world leader: someone who has the presence of mind to see what is approaching humanity from the future, to recognise the potential it hides, and to apply this in practice.

What is due to become physical reality first appears in the spirit. One might think that in that way everything is nicely lined up for us, that there exists something like predestination. In the previous chapter Jesse Mulder already went into the questions of what predestination is and how we can use our freedom. We will illustrate these questions with some practical examples.

So far, it looks as if coming events not only throw their shadows ahead, but also determine earthly reality. This applies to the natural world of mineral, plants and animals, to the extent that human beings do not disturb that world. Annie Gerding-Le Comte, who is known in Holland because of her publication about nature spirits, described this phenomenon many times.[3] For example, she describes how in the autumn, magnolia buds are already surrounded by the etheric image of the flowers of the coming season. On another occasion, just prior to a small tornado, she saw kobolds leaving their dwelling places to escape the approaching violence in nature.

This happens in the human world, too, but we are not as docile as plants and animals. On the contrary, our ego brings it about that providence often finds our door closed. Providence respects human freedom, our arbitrariness and obstinacy and, if necessary, waits with angelic patience for us to open the door to her.

The following is an illustration of the working of providence under impossible circumstances. This event took place in 1940 in Berlin. The Jewish poet Nelly Sachs needed to get out of Germany, where her fellow compatriots were disappearing one after another. The well-known Swedish author, Selma Lagerlöf, had invited her to Sweden. Everything was being done to get her a Swedish visa, but it was taking time. Nelly Sachs realised that something had to happen soon otherwise it would be too late to leave the country. One night she had a lucid dream. She saw herself as a white dove flying over the sea to Sweden. She could feel the strong wind pushing her back, and her wings were becoming heavier and heavier. She was losing altitude and was about to perish in the waves. Suddenly, she saw an eagle flying above her. Terrified she wanted to flee, but there was no escape. Then the eagle dove down, but instead of snatching her away as prey, it took her on its wings and carried her to the other side. The following day Nelly Sachs finally got her visa. The agent on duty urged her: 'You should go to the airport today; you should not wait any longer!' That is what she then did, and she was able to book the last flight to Sweden.

That is how providence works. In 'impossible conditions' a synergy of possibilities arises. Everything works together for the good. The dream Nelly Sachs had before her departure is an archetype we have known since antiquity. We have encountered it already in the chapter on the Apocalypse – 'The woman was given the two wings of the great eagle' (Rev. 12:14) – but the imagery goes further back than that. When Moses ascended Mount Sinai, the Godhead said to him, 'I carried you on eagles' wings and brought you to myself' (Ex. 19:4). Through many years' journey in the desert, Yahweh carried the Jewish people on eagles' wings. Using a different word we call this providence.

History repeats itself, but the imagery also goes through metamorphoses. In Chapter 12 of the Apocalypse it is not the eagle that carries the human being on its wings, but the human being gets her own wings: 'The woman was given the two wings of a great eagle, so that she might fly to the place prepared for her in the wilderness, where she would be taken care of for a time, times and half a time' (Rev. 12:14). The woman in the desert, a symbol of the loneliness of the human soul, is no longer carried by the Godhead, but has to find her own way to a place prepared by God.

Everything we do with true prayer and meditation gives us wings. How can we make this concrete? How can we develop a sense organ for what wants to come to us out of the world of providence?

First of all – and this seems self-evident – it needs time. I have to free up time to listen to that still voice, not just for a moment, not for a few days, but day in, day out, so that the spiritual world knows that I am knocking on the door. There are particular moments of the day that especially lend themselves to listening to the spiritual world: these are just before falling asleep and the moment of waking up.

At night we meet our guardian angel, who embodies providence in the most concrete sense of the word. Our angel not only has an overview of our whole life, but also goes with us from existence to existence. When we cultivate the silent moments of morning and evening, we connect day and night with our angel. In the evening we collect the harvest of the day to bestow it on the spiritual world at night; for that is where all our work on earth ultimately goes. The meeting with our angel at night gives us inspiration to do what is needed the following day – assuming we have ears to hear.

An old tradition in farming gives a classic example. Formerly when a farmer woke up he would keep his curtains closed for a little while as he pondered the impressions of the night in the semi-darkness of his room. There was a transition between sleeping and waking, a twilight condition in which he could take the harvest of the night into the day. Then only did the daily work begin. Similarly, there was also a custom after the work was finished to sit in silence on a bench in front of the house to ponder the events of the day – a form of review. These are pre-eminent moments to become open to what comes to us from the world of providence – assuming we have ears with which to hear.

There are many more forms of listening, although they do not work on their own. In a certain sense our feet are wiser than our head, but this wisdom only really shows itself when we put ourselves in the service of others. We don't have to follow the highest ideals for this to work; it is enough just to fulfil a modest task.

I was present at a remarkable example in a children's camp years ago. One of the young leaders had made a hut in the woods with his group of children, complete with an oven in which bread could be baked. On the day preceding the incident he had made a fire in that oven, and before he left, he put the fire out. The next morning, we went with the whole staff and all the children to the village to give a performance there. The leader who had made the fire in the hut the previous day suddenly walked away from the group and into the woods. He was of course responsible for his group of children, but something told him to go to the hut. There he saw that the heather was on fire. Although he had put the fire out the day before, the roots of the heather had smouldered and caught fire and now it was spreading. He was only just in time to call out a warning so that the fire could be put out.

For many years I worked with the young adults who lead these children's camps. We closed each day with a verse that described the different forms of listening that we practised:

Listen to the voices of those who went before us.
They prepared the way.
Their eyes are turned to the work of our hands.
Listen to the voice of your neighbour
Who seeks the redeeming words
To recognise his way amidst the detours.
Listen to the voices of the children,
Who are looking on unbeaten paths
For what wants to be born from the pains of the time.
Listen to the voice of your heart,
Which can only say in silence
Whence you come,
Whither you walk,
Who you are.

In our time, Otto Scharmer developed methods with his 'Theory U' to cultivate sense organs for the future.[4] His father, who had a biodynamic farm, taught him from his childhood the art of observing the field. He did that from time to time by walking into the field early in the morning and 'probing' what this field and this crop needed.

He applied this way of working in groups, beginning with the question, 'What do we need?' Scharmer calls this phase in the group process 'presencing'. We are living in a world in which we are often 'absent'. We don't want to take responsibility; we don't want to think. In his book *Theory U*, he gives methods for groups to develop this presence of mind.

To be able to lead an organisation out of the future requires three qualities: an open mind, an open heart, and an open will. By an open mind Scharmer means that we suspend judgment and put our prejudices aside, we say goodbye to all forms of fundamentalism and absolutism. Instead, we develop an open mind for possibilities we had not yet considered.

To cultivate an open heart we must try to put ourselves in the other's shoes. Too often our hearts are closed, focused only on ourselves. By this method, we make an effort to overcome that tendency.

Through an open will we make ourselves receptive to the will of the other, we interact with it. Every person, and also every organisation, has the tendency to cling to past results. But these offer no guarantees for the future; old solutions don't work anymore. We must learn to leave behind our own standpoints and explore what possibilities may exist together.

Through Otto Scharmer's work, a concept with which anthroposophy began – leading from the emerging future – is now applied in organisations. Scharmer calls this the development from an ego-system to an eco-system, in which all the elements and participants have their place. The key word in all phases of this developmental process is *listening*. And this means not only listening to what is articulated in a group of people, but also listening for what is not spoken. To help with this process Scharmer suggests a number of questions we can ask ourselves.

First of all, what wants to come into being in you?
Second, what difficulties do you face in making this happen?

Third, what gives you the most energy, what inspires you to achieve this?

He then suggests we take what he called 'a helicopter view'. Look down on your situation as if you were in a helicopter. What are you doing in this phase of your career or your biography? What are you trying to bring about? Or, if you are working for an organisation, what are you trying to bring about as a group?

Next comes a leap in time. Imagine you are in the last phase of your life. Have you done what you wanted to do? What did you want to leave behind here on earth?

When you have done this consider what advice you would give yourself now to make the next steps possible. How could you make that concrete? Do you have a vision, an intention, for the coming three to five years?

An important part of this process is learning to let go. What do you have to leave behind to make something possible? Do you have to let go of ideas that you have cultivated over the years? What is the old skin you have to cast off?

'Letting go' is followed by 'letting come', as you open up to what is coming towards you in the space you have created. As a result of this, the subsequent steps in the process become more and more concrete. Try to develop this as a prototype for the coming three months. Who are the people who can help you realise the picture you now have before you?

For the final step, ask yourself what practical steps you can take in the coming three days to make this possible.

To give an example of how such a group process unfolded, a few years ago seminary leaders were meeting in Stuttgart with a large group of students from three different training courses to discuss the future of these courses. The conclusion of this process was formulated as follows by one of the students: 'You teachers do not know how things should continue. We students do not know how things should continue. Only together are we able to discover, step-by-step, what the future of these courses will look like.'

A dramatic example of this group process was a situation a number of years ago in a psychiatric clinic where there were several cases of suicide. The executive staff realised that something had to happen, that they had to take action to turn the tide. The decision was made to consult with all the caregivers: the psychiatrist, the physician, the nurse, the eurythmist and the priest. Although none of them had a ready answer, step-by-step ideas grew as to what we could do to create a counterweight to the wave of suicides. We went to the spots where these suicides had taken place. A brief ritual was held, a prayer was spoken, there was eurythmy, and an address. Thus we went from one place to the next. Thereupon rest returned to the clinic.

What this situation demonstrated is how important it can be to act, to do something even when we're not sure what the next step is. Performing a constructive deed can help us avoid becoming paralysed, and in carrying it out the way forward often becomes clear. The physician Ita Wegman had this as her motto: the gods bend in action.

The gods can only work together with us when we act.

These days countless people feel overwhelmed with everything that is happening in the world and they feel that there is very little they can do to make a difference. This is a dangerous moment in the lives of individuals and societies, when the future can no longer become active because we ourselves do not act. We have to do something, perform a deed; then even fate can become providence.

There is all kinds of doom-laden speculation today about the fate that is awaiting our humanity, as if our collective destiny had already been decided. It is not the first time in history that large groups of people believe we are heading for an irrevocable end. There have been countless catastrophes before. Think of the cultures that once flowered, that were squashed and disappeared without a trace. Sooner or later every culture comes to an end. The question then is whether there will be enough people who are able to go through the eye of the needle and take the essence of such a culture into the future.

It was in this sense that Rudolf Steiner spoke to the founders of The Christian Community in September 1921: 'If humanity ends up in the abyss, there is for you only one possibility: that you go into the abyss with them and climb up again on the other side.' That was the task the priests were given, in full consciousness of coming catastrophes.

I end with an anecdote of a woman who had lost everything and did not know how to go on. Her husband had taken off with someone else and she had lost her job. She was completely thrown back onto herself. One morning, between sleeping and waking up, she heard a voice that inwardly, audibly said: 'What do you want to do? Do you want to swim or drown?' Vacillating, she said: 'I want to swim.' Upon which the voice sharply told her: 'Then do that!' Not only was it a serious voice that called her to order, but that voice also gave her the strength to pull herself out of the morass, to perform a deed and to take a new step in her life.

Only in the mysterious interplay between human hands and the hands of God can destiny find its way. It is no use us adopting a passive, almost fatalistic, attitude and expecting God to take care of everything for us. We are expected to act. God needs our hands; only then can something happen.

8

Providence: The Hidden Presence of Christ

The gentle powers shall surely win
in the end – I hear it as a heartfelt whispering
in me: if it were silent, all light would darken,
all warmth would freeze inside.

The powers that still fetter love
she will, slowly advancing, vanquish.
Then can the great beatitude begin
Which we, if our hearts harken with care,

hear soughing in all tenderness
as in little shells the great sea.
Love is the meaning of the life of planets

and humans and animals. There is nothing to disturb
the rising to her. And this is certain knowledge:
to perfect love everything will rise.

Henriette Roland-Holst (1869–1952)

Climatologists have spoken of climate change for a long time. Some time ago they began to use the term 'climate crisis', now they speak of a 'climate breach'. A breach has taken place in the way climate manifests itself, meaning that the usual models are no longer able to predict future developments. We are seeing more extreme weather events. In 2020 the World Nature Fund reported that not only has the number of wildfires been increasing, but they have also been more intense and lasted longer. In the past 35 years, the average duration of the wildfire season has increased by 19%. Along with this there is also the massive dying out of plant and animal species. In biology the term 'insect apocalypse' has been coined to indicate the kind of disaster that takes place when we lose insect species – let alone other animal species.[1]

We can think of nature today as a mirror of our conduct. When we see the dramatic phenomena happening around us, it is like looking in a mirror at the consequences of our deeds.

What is reflected in nature is also occurring in our social world. We are seeing an increasing polarisation of views with little common ground between them. The extremes are becoming more and more acute. And in our own souls, too, it can be incredibly hard to find that point of equilibrium, that inner balance. Most often this is the result of forces that work on us from outside. In our Western society the intellect and the will get extreme amounts of emphasis from our childhood on. The call for cognitive capacities and performance usually leads to a loss of the human middle, the qualities of the heart.

How can we cultivate the qualities of the heart in our time? 'It is only with the heart that one can see rightly,' says Antoine de Saint-Exupéry in his book *The Little Prince*. This brings us to the theme of this chapter: the hidden presence of Christ. This refers to the fact that Christ does not reside in some far-off, heavenly realm. He is right here with us on earth, but he is hidden from our ordinary sight. We therefore need to develop an organ of perception to discover him. As we grow more sensitive, we will see the many ways in which Christ manifests in the world around us and in our lives. I will describe four areas in which we can recognise this hidden presence for those who have eyes to see and ears to hear.

First of all, we can become attentive to the hidden presence of Christ in nature. We often look at nature as a product of the past: biologically speaking as the end product of evolution, and theologically speaking as an emanation of God. But the reality of nature is infinitely more complicated. The seventeenth-century mystic Angelus Silesius expressed in one of his verses how nature and the Trinity, expressed in the alchemical principles of salt, sulfur and mercury, are interwoven:

That God be three in one,
shows you each single herb
since sulfur, salt, and mercury
are seen together in one.[2]

In plants the *tria principia* of alchemy can be recognised: in the hard roots the salt principle, in the leaves and stalks the mobile mercury principle, and finally in the flowers and seed the fiery sulfur principle. The Father, who is the Ground of All Being, works in the salt processes. The Son, who mediates between heaven and earth, works in the mercury processes, while the Spirit works in the fiery sulfur processes. It is therefore possible to recognise in nature the hidden presence of Christ.

The twelfth-century Benedictine abbess Hildegard von Bingen, sometimes known as the 'walking encyclopedia' of the Middle Ages, discovered through study and meditation the forces that ceaselessly regenerate nature. In her time, Hildegard was a never-ending source of information for countless clerics, noblemen, princes and scholars. Not only did she become known for her visions of the origin and future of creation, but she was also able to put her knowledge and skills into practice in language, biology, medicine and music, among other disciplines.

Hildegard occupied herself especially with what she called the *Mysterium incarnationis*: the mystery of the embodiment, the Word made flesh. This is the actual theme of Christianity. Rather than seeing the physical world purely as *maya*, or an illusion, as some Eastern religions do, we must learn to recognise how the spirit works in matter. Goethe once said of his friend Schiller that he touched nothing without ennobling it. You might call this the hallmark of Christianity: cultivating the physical world with the aid of the spirit.

What did Hildegard von Bingen say about the mystery of the incarnation? She used an unusual phrase to indicate how Christ works in nature: *sancta viriditas*, the sacred green force. This is what she called the power of Christ at work in nature. Because of the Fall, said Hildegard, this green force (we might think of it as referring to 'vitality', but it is much more than that) has withered and become arid. When the time is fulfilled, however, Christ will appear again to awaken this aridity back to life.

Hildegard quoted a line from the New Testament to show what she meant with this. When Christ was led to Golgotha he said: 'If such things are possible while the tree is yet green, what may not happen when it is dry?' (Luke 23:31). Christ himself is the power of *viriditas* and if what happened at the crucifixion could be done to him who created life, what then would happen with the 'dry wood', with humanity when it has estranged itself from him?

According to Hildegard von Bingen, *viriditas* is the active force in all the processes of sprouting, rooting, growing, flowering and bearing fruit that we witness in nature. It is a concept that we also find in the alchemists of her time, who made use of this vital force in their work by collecting the dew on the plants in the early morning before sunrise. *Viriditas benedicta*, 'blessed growth force' is how Hildegard called this quintessence of nature, a term derived from the alchemists' *quinta essentia*, the fifth essence alongside the four essences of earth, water, air and fire popularly spoken of in antiquity.

Another author who wrote about this hidden presence was the poet Novalis, who went a step further than Hildegard von Bingen:

He is the star
He is the sun
He is the eternal source of life
From plant and stone and sea and light
Shines His divine countenance.

According to Novalis, the being that stood at the beginning of the creation – called the Logos, the creative Word, by John the Evangelist – appears in nature not only as a vital force, as *viriditas*, but as a countenance. This is the second way in which the hidden presence of Christ is at work in the world around us. He looks at us from every being of nature. How are we to understand this? Is it only a metaphor, a poetic liberty, or can we take it more literally? How does Christ observe us?

The gospels occasionally use a particular expression to indicate this. In the Gospel of Mark, when Christ meets the rich young man, the Evangelist writes, 'Jesus looked at him and loved him' (Mark 10:21), from the original Greek, *Iēsous emblepsas autōi ēgapēsen*. *Emblepsas* has the meaning of seeing into, seeing through. These two had never met before. It was literally love at first sight. Only it was not love in the sense of sympathy or friendship, but *agape*: the highest form of selfless love.

It is possible, however, that this look can affect us in a different way. The composer Richard Wagner described in his musical drama *Parsifal* how Kundry is persecuted by Christ's look after she laughed at him as he was being led to his crucifixion. She says to Parsifal:

> Through eternities I have waited for you, the saviour so late in coming, whom once I dared revile. Oh! If you knew the curse which afflicts me, asleep and awake, in death and life, pain and laughter, newly steeled to new affliction, endlessly through this existence! I saw Him – Him and mocked...! His gaze fell upon me! Now I seek Him from world to world to meet Him once again.[3]

The person who denied and mocked Christ is persecuted by his gaze her whole life. Kundry is the restless human being who, just like Ahasverus, has to wander homeless in eternity.

Associated with this idea of Christ observing us is how he reveals himself in the course of our lives. This is the third aspect. How can we discover the hidden presence of Christ in our biography?

Rudolf Steiner provides us with a way of discovering this guidance in his book *The Spiritual Guidance of the Individual and Humanity*. When we get older and look back on our lives, we may increasingly wonder at the course of events. In such a review we most often discover that we did things at a young age that we did not understand at the time, the meaning of which only now becomes recognisable. Steiner writes:

> Nevertheless, this sort of soul-searching is extraordinarily fruitful. For in such moments as we become aware that we are only now beginning to understand something we did in our earlier years … a new feeling emerges in our soul. We feel ourselves as if sheltered by a benevolent power presiding in the depths of our own being. We begin to trust more and more that, in the highest sense of the word, we are not alone in the world and that whatever we can understand or do consciously is fundamentally only a small part of what we accomplish in the world.[4]

What forces have been at work to create the composition of our life? Thornton Wilder gives an eloquent picture of this in one of his books, where he compares the course of human life with a woven tapestry. All our life we see the back of the tapestry, with its tangle of threads, its knots and loose ends, and it is only when our life is over and the tapestry turned around that we finally see the pattern created by the artist.

In this regard, Steiner draws special attention to a child's first three years, in which they learn to walk, speak and think. As we all know, in that period of life we are still like sleepwalkers. It is a great exception if people can remember the first moment when they could stand, walk, speak or think. Children are like marionettes that are carried and led by other forces. Think of the skill, art and wisdom needed to overcome gravity and to move out of the horizontal into the vertical. In this regard Steiner describes the connection small children have with the highest powers of the spiritual world:

In the first years of life … this higher wisdom functions like a 'telephone connection' to the spiritual beings in whose world we find ourselves between death and rebirth.[5]

Steiner goes on to say that, in these first three years, it is Christ who creates the capacities of walking, speaking and thinking. Children at this age are not yet subject to the powers of the adversary, unless terrible violence is committed in their surroundings. In themselves they are pure and innocent, and it is in this innocence that Christ works on and in each individual child.

Growing up means stumbling and falling and getting up again until you can stand on your own two feet. Spiritual adulthood is achieved through the uniquely human capacity of being able to give ourselves direction through self-knowledge. Through self-reflection, says Steiner, it is possible, particularly at a later age, to recognise Christ as leader in ourselves. We realise, he says: 'This is my inner guide.'[6] This reminds us of the opening line of Psalm 23: 'The Lord is my shepherd.'

One of the founders of The Christian Community, Heinrich Ogilvie, wrote a free rendering of Psalm 23. In this version it becomes evident who the real shepherd is:

Christ is my guide.
Nothing shall I fear.
He leads me throughout life,
He is the strength in all my works,
He comforts me in life's suffering
And in my darknesses shines His light.
Though I go through the valley of death,
I fear no evil
For You are with me.
Your hand shows me the way.
You raise the table for me

With sustenance for my eternal being.
You anoint my head with oil
And spirit courage flows
From the cup of suffering.
Yes, Your strength lives in my weakness
And Your life vanquishes my dying.
You build with might in me
The new human being.

This experience of spiritual guidance is described by the French nurse and playwright Gabrielle Bossis in her diaries. Starting in her fiftieth year she had inner conversations with Christ. On September 16, 1948, she wrote in her diary the following words Christ spoke to her:

When a stranger travels through a far country it always hurts when he never meets a friendly eye, and the way becomes a torment for him. I am this stranger when no thought of me fills your souls, when your souls are closed and without life. Then I call you through small events, through a circumstance, and you will say: that was a coincidence. Who of you will say: 'It is He?'[7]

This was how Gabrielle Bossis heard the voice of Christ, who, as Lord of karma, accompanies each human being on their way through life.

The fourth area in which the hidden presence of Christ can be discerned is in social situations. This is often hard to find, especially when we are caught up in situations where extreme points of view dominate and no middle ground can be found between people. Nevertheless, in such conflicts it is still possible to find the golden middle, even though this demands much from both sides.

In my forty years as a priest, I have had plenty of opportunities, by trial and error, to resolve such conflicts. I was in the fortunate position to be sent three times to the same Christian Community congregation in Zeist, with gaps in between when I was working elsewhere. In the 1980s I met a woman in the congregation who had been severely traumatised by the Second World War and by her work in the resistance movement. She led a reclusive life and was bedridden for her final years. The first time she met me, she said: 'You can only help me if you imagine that the Christ is between you and me.' Here I was encountering a situation that was very different from my own. I was in the prime of life, I had started a new profession and had a young family. This woman on the other hand lived a reclusive existence and was chronically ill. From these totally different standpoints we had to find our way through numerous confrontations that, all together, lasted for twenty years until her death. When after many years we had finally found the middle, we both recognised the Christ. Under the impression of this experience, I wrote the following poem:

> You were a stranger to me
> whose tongue I did not comprehend.
> I had to practice silence
> until the word would find its way.
> So long have I listened,
> and you to me,
> till we could in our silence hear
> what never yet was spoken:
> a silence in which the future is born.
> In stillness it wove between you and me –
> That was He,
> That was He.

It has been my intention in this chapter to indicate that the reality in which we live is different from the physical events that happen to us. These events may well demand our attention, but they also prevent us from seeing the true reality.

Willem Zeylmans van Emmichoven, a pioneer of anthroposophy

in The Netherlands, wrote: 'At a certain stage of my development I came to the inner realisation that Christ is the reality in which we live.'[8] Whoever has discovered the truth of this will find Christ not only in the kind of still moments I have described from my own experience, but also in crisis and confrontation. Of course, it is a difficult task to recognise his presence when the water is rising to our necks, and yet, when the worst is behind us and we have gone through the eye of the needle, we are often surprised at the course events have taken. We may live in a world of chaos, but there is still someone who can bring order to the chaos. And even that chaos – which we would rather ignore or avoid – may be the work of the Lord of destiny.

Thus says Christ in the Letter to Laodicea: 'Those whom I love I rebuke and discipline. So be earnest and repent' (Rev. 3:19). The entire Apocalypse is one succession of blows of destiny and trials which, paradoxical as it may sound, are an expression of divine love. This paradox comes to expression already during the life of Christ in his own words. The weakness, the sluggishness and the indifference of human beings bring him from time to time to despair: 'You unbelieving and perverse generation. How long shall I stay with you? How long shall I put up with you?' (Matt. 17:17).

And yet he decided to take on the unbearable – not for a short time, but for always – when after his resurrection he gave the redeeming answer to his desperate question: 'And surely I am with you always, to the very end of the age' (Matt. 28:20).

'Behold, I Make All Things New': Morality As Creative Principle

Jesse Mulder

Then I saw 'a new heaven and a new earth', for the first heaven and the first earth had passed away, and there was no longer any sea. I saw the Holy City, the new Jerusalem, coming down out of heaven from God, prepared as a bride beautifully dressed for her husband.

Rev. 21:1–2

We human beings are moral beings. All that we do is a matter of moral consideration. This distinguishes us from the realms of nature around us, from stones and plants and animals. That seems self-evident. But when you look at the kinds of things that make the rounds in our current cultural context, it turns out not to be so self-evident at all. For instance, my attention was recently drawn to a podcast about the future of the earth and humanity.[1] It speaks about a variety of social movements that attempt to lessen suffering in the world as a step towards a morally better future, among them are those concerned for the wellbeing of animals in the wild.

One episode focuses on a scientific article called 'Policing Nature'.[2] The idea behind the article is that not only do *we* cause suffering in the animal kingdom, but animals themselves are not particularly kind to each other either. Therefore, if it is our goal to lessen suffering in the animal world, we would also have to keep the pike from gobbling up little ducklings, the lion from killing the antelope. If it were possible then we would have to put all predators on a vegan diet.

That is, of course, an absurdity. It demonstrates how current thinking about morality can become so distorted precisely because we lose sight of the fact that morality belongs to the domain of human beings. It is *our* way of dealing with animals, the suffering *we* cause them, that must be a subject of moral consideration, but the pike and the lion are not bound to moral reflection in that way. The falcon that takes a field mouse does not reflect on the suffering it causes the field mouse and its family. Nature takes its course and there can be no question of morality here; nature is a totally amoral sphere.

Effective Altruism is the name of one of the movements working in the direction described above. 'Effective altruists' try to commit their capacities and resources as effectively as possible to eliminate poverty and suffering from the world. Leading figures in this movement, such as the Australian-British ethicist Toby Ord, give large parts of their income to good causes.[3] Young people are encouraged to start lucrative careers with the objective of being able to donate as much as possible to organisations that affect positive change.

In the context of these movements there is also scientific research into which causes are most effective in preventing suffering and pain. For example, in his book *The Most Good You Can Do*, the influential animal ethicist Peter Singer says that it may make more difference for the alleviation of suffering in the world if we stop raising chickens than it would if we managed to lessen human poverty. You notice in his way of thinking a scientific approach to moral questions: there are n chickens in chicken farms that, on average, each go through a quantity k of suffering, so that the total quantity of suffering among chickens is $n \times k$. Because there are at least 25 billion chickens on the earth, the total amount of suffering among chickens will be much higher than the total suffering of people who live in poverty – even if we estimate the suffering of one person in poverty to be much higher than that of one chicken in a chicken farm. In that way morality is distorted into a purely quantitative issue.

In my view such an ethical movement suffers from a certain tunnel vision when it comes to morality. In its preoccupation with how much suffering is caused or alleviated, it restricts the possibilities for a meaningful orientation in life. This becomes abundantly clear when we ask what is it that underpins such a movement. What is its goal? We realise that it is striving to create a kind of utopia on earth, one in which there is no suffering and no illness anymore, where all pain and discomfort can be alleviated with a pill, where everyone is constantly happy and carefree, and where no one, human being or animal, is ever hurt.

But if we try to imagine what this might look like, we soon realise that it's meaninglessness. No true development is possible in such a utopia, for all development has come to a standstill.

That sense of meaninglessness is due to the fact that Effective Altruism, like all similar movements, is wholly based on the modern scientific image of the human being and the world. You could formulate the idea underlying it as follows: 'I am an accidental, temporary inhabitant, a puny piece of dust in an enormous, dead, material world that is determined by blind laws of nature.' That whole, enormous material universe has no goal and no development.

It is worth emphasising that this is the fundamental feeling that our modern time cultivates in the souls of *all* people, simply because we all grow up in our current cultural circumstances. From this point of view, it makes no difference for the universe whether or not we humans exist at all. That is no more than a coincidence. The only thing that can then give us a moral direction is the immediate experience of pleasure and suffering, joy and pain. Pleasure is fine, joy is good; suffering, pain and illness are all bad. And that is the limit of our moral concerns.

However, this has no significance for your individual development or the development of humanity, let alone the development of the earth and the cosmos. When considered in this way, morality has no significance at all beyond joy and pain. If you are an egoist, you only consider your *own* pleasure and suffering; if you are an altruist, you are concerned with the pleasure and discomfort of others. From this materialistic perspective, moral progress consists in increasing the circle of your altruism, the circle of other people to whom you commit yourself. Whereas this circle may at first include only your immediate family, it can grow to encompass friends, colleagues, neighbours, and yes, all people, even animals. But it continues to be exclusively about pleasure and suffering. That is the extent of this modern, materialistic morality.

Of course, there is nothing wrong with helping others who are in trouble, with alleviating suffering, and with a better distribution of prosperity. There is also nothing wrong with taking care of animals and with challenging abusive practices in our food industry. All of that can be part of a meaningful moral orientation in life. But that is different from a moral attitude that strives for these things *exclusively* because pleasure and suffering are the *only* things that matter morally.

The law of the conservation of energy

Let us now connect this exploration of a modern, scientifically based approach to morality with something Rudolf Steiner mentioned a surprising number of times, namely the law of the conservation of energy.

This law of the conservation of energy is a fundamental law of our current physics and states that the total amount of energy at the beginning of a process is equal to the total amount of energy at the end of the process – it is *conserved* over time. A simple example of this is when we drive a car. When we start the engine and press down on the accelerator, the car begins to move. Movement is a form of kinetic energy (from the Greek word *kinesis,* movement) and this energy is provided by the car's engine, which takes the chemical energy stored in the fuel and, through a process of controlled combustion, transforms it into movement. Not all of the energy is transformed into movement, however, as part of it is lost through heat. But if we take this into account, then the total amount of energy remains constant throughout. The total amount of energy that was contained in the gasoline in chemical form is the same amount that now results in movement and warmth.

The amount of matter also remains constant, although it assumes a different form – instead of fuel we now have exhaust fumes. With Einstein's famous formula $E = mc^2$, which makes a connection between energy (E) and mass (m), we can ultimately even say that energy and mass are interchangeable. We can therefore speak of a universal law of the conservation of mass and energy. This is of course a very simplified representation of the matter, but it suffices for my purposes here.

Steiner was critical of this law, calling it a 'great stumbling-block to any understanding of man'.[4] The reason why he said this becomes clear when you consider the implications of this law more deeply. According to this law, the total amount of matter/energy always stays the same: nothing is ever lost, nothing is ever added. And whatever form it takes, in its essence it remains the same through all time. In other words, energy/matter is eternal and only its configuration, its form, is temporary. This even includes our human existence and everything we do.

Thus we come back to what I characterised as the fundamental feeling of our modern, scientific time, which sees human existence as an accidental event and human beings as temporary inhabitants of a purely material world determined by blind laws of nature. All things considered, that is a rather depressing thought.

This law of the conservation of energy encompasses the essence of materialism and gives rise to a sense of meaninglessness for all that we as human beings are and do. For this law leads to the view that what is eternal and imperishable is not the spirit, but dead, purposeless, blind matter.

Morality as creative power

Let us now return to a brief but significant saying of Christ from the Little Apocalypse that was mentioned in Chapter 4: 'Heaven and earth will pass away, but my words will never pass away' (Matt. 24:35). If we compare these words to the law of the conservation of energy and matter, we will have to conclude that they represent a complete rejection of this law. The whole perspective is completely turned around. The energy/matter that makes up the material world is not pictured as imperishable, but rather the opposite, as temporary. And it is the word of Christ, who after all is the Logos, the Word of Worlds, that remains and is eternal.

We can connect these words with the Book of Revelation, in which we are shown a picture of the passing away of heaven and earth. When all the trials and catastrophes are past and the New Jerusalem, the new world, makes its appearance from on high, Christ then says: 'Behold, I make all things new' (Rev. 21:5). The Greek text here says, *'idou* [meaning 'see', 'behold'] *kaina poiō panta'*. The verb *poiein* means 'to make' or 'create', *panta* means 'all things', and *kaina* means 'new' or 'fresh' and indicates what this creating signifies for the whole creation.

As has already been pointed out in Chapter 5 on the Apocalypse, the Greek language has two words for 'new': *neos* and *kainos*. *Neos* often appears in our language as a prefix, as in neogothic and neoliberalism. It indicates that something is being repeated, perhaps in a slightly different form and in a different context, but it still refers to something that has already existed. *Kainos*, however, indicates a more radical kind of newness. It indicates the transition to something completely new that was not there before.

We therefore look towards this distant future when all that is outer nature, including all that we have become as human beings, will completely pass away and yet, at the same time, will also contain the seed of that new world, the New Jerusalem. In his cosmology, Rudolf Steiner calls this new step in the development of the earth and humanity the Jupiter phase and describes it as a subsequent incarnation of our earth and solar system.

This calls forth the question: what is that seed that contains the power to grow into the coming Jupiter planet of human evolution?

All matter, all that is sensory and external, will pass away. We could say that this is the seed-covering that withers and falls away when the new germ unfolds. What remains and forms the germ, however, is our morality, and this can only be found in human beings.

If we take this thought deeply into us, then the materialistic feeling described above can be totally transformed into a more spiritual feeling. We realise that the current physical earth is a temporary phase in which moral forces can be laid down, in and by ourselves, as the foundation for a new world. This is the transformation of materialism into spiritualism – matter is temporary, spirit is eternal. Human beings thus appear in their essence as eternal beings, and the earth as a temporary home that will eventually pass away. Furthermore, the earth only makes sense and has meaning to the extent that human beings succeed in laying the seeds for a new world in it.

The contrast with the modern materialistic view of morality is enormous. Whereas this modern world view ascribes no significance to the development of the earth and its inhabitants, a spiritual perspective shows us that our morality is the key factor for the future of the earth. For it is our morality that remains after all that is material has fallen away. Whereas our anthroposophical perspective of the significance of morality is future oriented, the ethics of materialism, with its focus on pleasure and suffering, is oriented towards purely earthly conditions, to those forces and substances that will irrevocably pass away as the era of our current earth comes to an end.

Old Moon, Earth, Jupiter: the development and demise of the world

From an all-encompassing eagle's perspective, we have now formed a picture of the earth in its current form of existence: the physical, outer world in which we live; a temporary dwelling place that will eventually fall away and wither like the seed within which the germ was able to ripen. Out of the morality that we human beings develop, a new world will make its appearance, a world which, down to its physical constitution, will be completely new – *kainos*.

With this perspective in mind, we might turn our gaze in the opposite direction and ask: what is the origin of the material world that now surrounds us? Whereas current science, reasoning out of the law of the conservation of energy and matter, argues in linear fashion back to the past and thus arrives at pictures like the Big Bang, based on the principle we have now discovered, we would have to say that the whole physical-sensory world comes from moral seeds that were sown in a still earlier phase of development. Indeed, several wisdom traditions describe that in the evolution of the world and humanity, there was a phase that preceded our current earth. In anthroposophy, this phase is called Old Moon. At that time, human beings had not yet reached the stage when they could develop morality themselves. Therefore, the moral seeds that were planted in that phase, and which underlie our current earthly environment, were sown by beings from the angelic hierarchies.

It would be natural to conclude from this that this is how development always goes. A world comes into being in which moral seeds are formed that subsequently become the basis for a new world, and thus world arises from world every time. But if we think this way then we end up thinking like our natural scientists do now, who simply project forwards and backwards in time what they have developed as a science of matter. Such projections do not lead to concrete insights. What can be helpful is if we consider another important spiritual law, which states that development always means *differentiation*. This holds true both in the macrocosm and the microcosm. In different eras of human development different qualities unfold themselves. In the distant past, during the cultural epoch of Ancient India, the quality of complete surrender to the divine was developed, individuals erased themselves as it were. In our time, however, it is exactly the individual who takes centre stage. In our time we are experiencing the pinnacle of individualism, and with it we also unfold our freedom as I described in the chapter on freedom and inevitability. This individual freedom obviously cannot be developed concurrently with surrender to the divine, and so, in order to bring these qualities to maturity, differentiation in development is necessary. First one aspect is developed, then another at a later stage. In this we can sense the wise guidance of humanity that was described in the last chapter.

This law of differentiation also applies in the evolution of the earth out of Old Moon. The emergence and decline of whole worlds is never a *repeat*, for what could be developed on Old Moon was something very different from what we now have to develop on the earth as seeds for the coming Jupiter phase, for the New Jerusalem.

Rudolf Steiner described it as follows in his book *Occult Science*:[5] on Old Moon the spiritual hierarchies worked in such a way that this planet eventually developed into a 'cosmos of wisdom'. Wisdom was developed as an essential, moral element, and it is this wisdom that we now see in the world around us. All we need do is to look at some phenomenon in nature and we will see how it is permeated with wisdom. The epitome of this wisdom can be found in the wise construction of the human body. Thus, what was first developed as an inner, moral quality on Old Moon, later became visible in our outer environment.

What is now the task of our current Earth phase? It is not wisdom, for then nothing new, nothing *kainos*, would come into being. Instead, it is love: pure, spiritualised love. It is our mission here on earth to unfold that kind of love so that the current phase of development will give rise to a 'cosmos of love'. And just as the wisdom developed on Old Moon now appears all around us in nature, the love that we develop here on earth as the core of our moral striving will in its turn become visible in the natural surroundings on Jupiter.

Destruction in the human being

We now have this great perspective of the future of the earth stretching before us. We see how the outer materiality will wither and fall away like the seed-cover surrounding the germ, and that this germ will contain what we human beings have been able to develop through our morality, a morality that can ultimately be expressed in the word love.

We can now connect this great perspective with the law of the conservation of energy and matter. I have already mentioned that Rudolf Steiner spoke critically about this law, and we can understand why based on the perspective we have arrived at of cosmic evolution. For this law turns everything upside down: that which is temporary, the outer material world, is declared imperishable, while that which is eternal, the human spirit that is continually developing, is deemed to be merely temporary. But that is not the only problem. The reason Steiner said this law is an obstacle to understanding human beings is because it is precisely in human beings that the law does not hold true.

In human beings, and *exclusively* in human beings, matter is truly destroyed. In human beings, therefore, complete conservation of energy and matter does not exist. Steiner even speaks of a 'source of destruction' existing within us: 'Within the human being, matter is completely dissolved into nothingness. The very essence of matter is fully destroyed.'[6] He then explains that it has to be that way. If we want to develop an autonomous, clear-thinking I, this is only possible if forces are at work that are so strong that matter is indeed destroyed.

However, these forces do not work in our head, in our waking consciousness, but in the opposite pole of our being, which has to do with our metabolism and will. This counter pole is separated from our consciousness; we are completely unaware of it. You could say that, whereas in our head we develop clear, sober earth consciousness, in our middle area around our diaphragm, there is something like a cover that keeps these destructive processes out of our normal consciousness. Or, as Steiner himself expressed it, there is a mirror that, when we look inward, reflects back our memories, but *behind it* lies that source of destruction. If we have gained the strength for it through inner development we can, as it were, pierce through that memory-mirror, and then we can see the tremendous 'fury of destruction' that is working deep within us.[7]

Now, this source of destruction in our lower pole is of fundamental importance for our moral development. From there all kinds of lower impulses and passions rise up which, on the one hand, give us our egoity, our strong feeling of I, but on the other can also make us very egotistic when we strengthen our I at the expense of others and our environment. If we allow these impulses to lead us, then we become immoral individuals. But if we permeate this source of destruction with moral impulses, if we let love guide us in our will and our deeds, then we overcome what pulls us down. We transform the power that exists there and thus we become moral individuals. In this way we can connect the destruction of matter very concretely with the moral work that we are to do here on earth as human beings.

This source of destruction in the core of our being makes it possible that the new, the moral, can be made into a reality. And that is understandable in the light of the foregoing. The old, that which has become, earthly matter, has to give way, and the forces it contains have to be freed, so that the new can be planted in them. In Steiner's own words:

In this source of destruction ... matter is truly annihilated.
Matter is thrown back into its nothingness, and then we allow,

within this nothingness, the good to arise. The good can arise if, instead of our instincts and impulses, which are bound to work towards the cultivation of egoity, we pour into this source of destruction, by means of a moral inclination of soul, all moral and ethical ideals. Then something new arises. Then in this very source of destruction the seeds of future worlds arise. Then we, as human beings, take part in the coming into being of worlds ... In the Jupiter existence there will be only the new creation that already is being formed today in the human being out of moral ideals, within this source of destruction.[8]

Of course, not only what we develop as good moral deeds will become seeds for the future Jupiter phase, but also our anti-moral and egotistic deeds arising out of this source of destruction. These will not be moral seeds of love, but immoral seeds of hatred and isolation. We can therefore see that the development of morality will not be finished even with the transition to the future Jupiter phase. On Jupiter, the natural world will not only manifest love, but also what we are currently developing in the way of immorality.

The Jupiter phase will also bring with it its own moral tasks, which will ultimately lead to the transition to another phase, the Venus phase as it is called in anthroposophy. Development is always ongoing and is always new – *kainos*.

It truly depends on human beings and our moral development what the future Jupiter world will look like. Morality is the creative principle, but it is a real possibility that immorality will become mixed up with it as a disrupting element.

The earth forms the stage on which human beings go through their development to become autonomous, individual I-beings. The fundamental challenge in our moral development is that we achieve this autonomy without closing ourselves off from our spiritual development, without isolating ourselves and becoming egotists. Love is the power that makes this possible because we can only develop love for something or someone if there is a distinction: I am over here and the being towards which my love goes is over there. While, from this point of view, love relies on the distinction between the one who loves and the one who is loved, love is at the same time that which overcomes this distinction. If our love is pure and without passion, then this love creates in us a space not only for our individual selves, but also for the other, the one whom we love. When we realise that Christ is the teacher of this human love, we realise the importance of Paul's words: 'Not I, but Christ in me' (Gal. 2:20). This is the entire significance of our moral development on earth.

The interior of the earth

We can deepen these connections even more. We know that human beings are a microcosm in the macrocosm, a little world that is a reflection of the big world, the cosmos. And thus we might wonder what corresponds on that large scale with the 'source of destruction' in the human being described above.

To find this macrocosmic correspondence it is helpful to take another look at the source of destruction. It isolates us from the world by awakening strong impulses in us that make us aware of ourselves as separate beings. When we strongly experience desire for something, this feeling strengthens our egoity, our awareness of ourselves as separate, autonomous beings. This effect is necessary for the development of our I-consciousness.

What then is it that works similarly on the large scale? The answer is quickly found. It is the earth itself, our planet, which places itself as an autonomous body in the cosmos and offers us a dwelling place upon which we can develop our independence.

Is there then in the earth also a kind of a source of destruction? To answer that question, we first have to go back to April 5, 1906, and the eruption of Mount Vesuvius that largely destroyed the Italian city of Naples. As it turned out, this event made a deep impression on Rudolf Steiner, who in the subsequent months shared profound insights in his lectures about the hidden interior of our planet earth.[9] In these lectures Steiner described nine layers that make up the interior of the earth. We are walking around on the uppermost, mineral layer, as investigated by our sciences. But, according to Steiner, this layer is just a shell, like that of an egg. Below it, things are very different. If you would go down into the deeper layers – which, looking at it from the outside, is completely impossible – even matter has a completely different nature.

There is no need to consider the nine layers here; it suffices instead to mention that these deeper layers of the earth constantly emanate a destructive, negative activity.[10] For example, the substances that make up the first two layers below the mineral one turn out to be inimical to life and to have a destructive effect on all experience. Still deeper lies a substance that shows a kind of rampant life, like that of a cancer tumour, and below that we find a layer of a substance that consists of violent passions and desires.

But what is of special interest for us, however, is the layer close to the core of the earth. The eighth layer, known in occult science as the divisive layer or the fragmenter, and its essential nature is that it disrupts and destroys moral qualities. The forces this layer sends up to the earth's surface cause conflict and disharmony on the earth.

There is a mysterious connection between the source of destruction in ourselves, which contains the forces that isolate us in our I-consciousness, and this 'divisive layer', which is close to the core of the earth. There is also a mysterious connection between what we can do to sow moral seeds for the future and transform this source of destruction in ourselves, and the interior of the earth. 'For,' Steiner continues, 'people have to work together in harmony to overcome the divisive force of this earth layer.' In similar ways all other negative qualities of the various earth layers can be overcome by the development of humanity:

Man transforms his dwelling place and himself at the same
time, and when he spiritualizes himself, he spiritualizes the
earth also. One day, at a later planetary stage, he will have
ennobled the earth by his own creative power. Every moment
when we think and feel, we are working on the great structure
of the earth.[11]

With this kind of view of the interior of the earth we can hardly
fail to think of Holy Saturday, the day when Christ descends into the
interior of the earth and brings it his light.

'Behold, I make all things new.' This is the ultimate result of
Christ's working on earth, and our moral development will ultimately
coincide with it, for where we sow seeds of love for the future phase
of world evolution, Christ works with us and in us. The source of
destruction within our own being will then be illuminated by Christ's
love, and the dark interior of the earth transformed into illuminating
spirit. In this way we help to build something truly new – *kainos* –
and thereby transform the earth itself.

10

Our Self-created Destiny

The tremendous difference from earlier ways will be that human beings and not principles or institutions are the active agent ... Setting up programs is something that belongs to the past. The future depends on the existence of people who act in the right way out of their own resources.

Rudolf Steiner

The subject of the previous chapter was once summed up by Rudolf Steiner in a single sentence: 'Human souls must be strong enough to bring good out of evil through a process of spiritual alchemy.'[1] This sentence could also be applied to the theme of this chapter. Alchemy is the art of transforming the material world through transubstantiation: matter, which has become separated from its spiritual origin, is connected once again with this origin and is gradually transformed back into spirit. You might also say that alchemy is like composting evil until it has been changed into something good.

In the lecture quoted at the start of this chapter, Steiner explains that the forces that determine the future do not derive from some external authority but are connected with our own morality: 'The future resides in the hearts of men and women.'[2] Everything that is now in us in the form of thoughts, emotions, feelings and impulses becomes our environment in the distant future. We can also say: everything that is in us eventually becomes our destiny. In that way it is also expressed in a verse that is attributed to the Buddha:

The thought manifests as the word,
The word manifests as the deed,
The deed develops into habit,
And the habit hardens into character.

So watch the thought and its way with care,
And let it spring from love
Born out of concern for all beings.

What begins with our thoughts becomes in the long run our destiny. Human beings are free to choose between good and evil. Right now, we can still hide our intentions and proclaim a lie that fools everyone. But a time is coming, says Rudolf Steiner in this lecture, when everything we think will be written on our forehead and imprinted in our body. It will become our physiognomy. Everything we think, speak and do will eventually become the physiognomy of the earth around us.

When Rudolf Steiner gave this lecture in 1906 it was perhaps not yet so evident what he meant. I have the impression that in our time this is slowly coming to light. Children and young people today are often able to hear right through the words and outer appearance to what the actual intention is of the person who is speaking and acting.

The head of a large school told me some years ago how he evaluated candidates who applied for a teaching position. He said: 'I pay less attention to outer aspects, such as order, discipline, didactics, or use of language. Most important for me is that the applicant shows himself as he is, without outer show. I don't listen primarily to what he says, but how he says it. What is his intention? What is the moral music that is sounding through it?'

In his lecture about morality and the future, Steiner used a loaded term which, however, has nothing to do with outer characteristics:

A new race will be formed that will constitute the connecting
link between present-day humanity and the spiritualised
human being of the future. But one must distinguish between
the evolution of races and the evolution of souls ... Individuals
will belong to this race only through the exercise of their
free will and through a great exertion of their soul forces.
Membership in a race will no longer be forced upon a soul,
but rather it will be the result of an individual's evolution.[3]

Steiner was not speaking here about physical races, but about
a moral distinction that would make itself increasingly apparent
between large numbers of individuals. This same theme also runs
through the Apocalypse like a red thread. Part of humanity lets itself
be guided by selfless impulses; another part becomes trapped in
materialism and egoism. According to Steiner:

From now on, souls should prepare themselves to transform
into good the evil that will appear in its full strength in the
sixth epoch.[4]

That is spiritual alchemy, in which evil is transformed into
good. The sixteenth-century mystic Jacob Böhme expressed this
transformation in the following way: 'The worst must be the cause
of the best.'[5] We encounter this idea in countless forms of predictions
and prophecy: before the good can triumph, evil has to culminate.

We human beings are not the only ones who are to some extent
free to do what we want. The adversarial forces also receive latitude
to expand their power. And it is not their show of power, nor the
violence they unleash that is decisive, but our own morality working
in harmony with the leading powers of the spiritual world. It is the
element of the free will that implies that the future is not cast in stone.
Radically formulated: we *are* the future – for good or for evil.

At the same time, the future is, imaginatively speaking, already present – it is *in statu nascendi*, in the process of being born. The motif of the future physiognomy, described by Rudolf Steiner in the lecture mentioned above, appears in the Apocalypse in the multitude of the 144,000, who receive the seal of God on their foreheads: the servants of God (Rev. 7:3). To form a concrete picture of these servants, it is helpful to realise how the circle of twelve disciples came about.

Christ recognised each one of them at first sight – 'Follow me.' Of some he said that they were prepared for their future task and had already come a long way. Thus he said of Nathanael: 'Here is a true Israelite, in whom there is nothing false' (John 1:47). Christ 'composed' a circle of twelve pupils who made it possible for him to form a community. The Gospel of Mark twice uses the unconventional words 'He made twelve' – *epoiēsen dōdeka* (Mark 3:14 and 16). Thus he also composed the future community of all communities, which is qualitatively expressed in the number 144,000 (12 x 12,000). The well-known fact that no human being is completely predictable means that even the initiate is unable to describe the future in all its details. To some extent the future remains an enigma.

Friedrich Rittelmeyer, who had a number of profound conversations with Rudolf Steiner, once asked him many questions about the predictability of the future: 'Have you really never been mistaken in your investigations and been obliged to correct them afterwards?' Steiner replied: 'I have never spoken of what I wasn't quite sure of.' Rittelmeyer was not satisfied: 'Have you not on closer scrutiny had to correct your first impression and results of research?' Steiner replied: 'Yes, but then there is always an obvious reason for it. For instance, if I meet you in the fog and do not recognise you, the fog itself is a factor which must be taken into account.' Rittelmeyer was still not satisfied: 'Has it never happened that you had to admit afterwards, "I was wrong there."?' Steiner thought quietly for a moment or two, then replied: 'Well, yes, in human beings I have sometimes been deceived. But after all, with people, something from outer life will often creep in that one cannot foresee.'[6]

In the fourth mystery drama, *The Soul's Awakening*, a moment occurs when Strader, the man of science, has indefinite impressions of his future karma. He is near the end of his life and he feels stuck and at a stand-still. The veil obscuring his future destiny is briefly lifted and he sees himself in a big rowing boat. At the helm is the initiate, Benedictus. Strader is at the oars and is rowing. Then another ship approaches with his opponents, and to his consternation he sees that Ahriman is at the helm. That ship approaches him at full speed, and a collision seems imminent.

Facing this dire picture Strader asks Benedictus: 'Am I then armed and strong enough to fight?' In his answer Benedictus speaks not about a lucid insight, but only about a feeling.

BENEDICTUS: I feel that you can strengthen still the power
which showed the image to your spirit eyes.
And I can also see, you will create
new forces for yourself and your friends,
if only you will rightly strive for strength.
This I can sense. How it will come to pass
remains a secret hidden from my sight.[7]

This dramatic scene shows an element that is to a certain extent recognisable for almost every human being. For we all have more or less indeterminate feelings about the future.

The biggest riddle is karma, our self-created destiny. What we think, speak and do eventually becomes our destiny. Thankfully, we are never completely alone in this. We have, thank God, fellow sufferers who cross our path, and how they cross our path is a riddle in its own right. Fortunately, our feet are wiser than our head. They take us on their own to our fellow sufferers.

Years ago, impressed by the miracle of the human encounter and the karmic 'companions' who run into each other in life, I wrote the following poem:

We travel together on one ship
So do we wander on the sea.
We travel together with one light
A star is going with us.
Darkness comes to meet us
But no one goes alone
We will do battle if we must.
Not one will become lost.
No one knows the water that awaits us.
The sea'll be all around us.
As dark as night is destiny
But we, we stay together.

In Rudolf Steiner's lectures, certain terms and key words occur frequently. Not surprisingly, 'human being' is one of them, often used to describe anthroposophy, as is 'development'.[8] The essence of anthroposophy is that everything that happens in our lives offers us a possibility to develop ourselves, even if it happens through a catastrophe. In Chapter 7, I mentioned the radical expression Rudolf Steiner used in his course for the priests in September 1921: 'If humanity ends up in the abyss, there is for you only one possibility: that you go into the abyss with them and climb up again on the other side.'[9]

That things go from bad to worse is no reason for pessimism but should serve as a stimulus to guide our actions and give us direction for the future. The best preparation for this is to become free and independent, not only in the outer sense of the word, but also independent in our thinking. In a lecture he gave on October 8, 1906, Rudolf Steiner discussed the moral impulses that create the future. As long as these impulses come from the outside in the form of precepts that compel us, they have no significance for the future. Only individual freedom, says Steiner, opens the door to the spiritual world for people, and gives us a future perspective.

At the same time, this individual freedom also brings arbitrariness and chaos. Notwithstanding, he calls this development necessary: 'We perceive chaos in our civilisation. That is true. Theoretically speaking, materialism holds chaos in it.'[10]

If we want to invest spiritually in the future, we should know that results achieved in the past do not give any guarantee for the future. Everything given as solutions in the past – in social life, economic life and the life of rights – is no longer useful for the future. We have to dare to live out of this chaos principle.

Here we see the good side even of chaos. If our civilisation had not fallen into chaos, we would not have been able to develop ourselves freely out of our own resources. We would have always been bound to our environment. The old order must therefore break apart, become chaos. We face great changes in this respect, and no one can hope to reform anything in the world except by means of inner development. Anything else would be amateurish prophecy.

Here the key word development sounds again. The only thing that counts is the personal development of every soul. Also, in the confrontation with evil it is necessary to preserve our autonomy by using our common sense. How do we learn to discriminate between good and evil?

In his *Nicomachean Ethics*, Aristotle explained how the good is found, and creates the golden middle, between two extremes. For example, between greed and wastefulness balance is found in generosity and temperance. Between materialism and spiritual ecstasy we find balance through sobriety and idealism, through remaining grounded whilst still being open to inspiration and new possibilities. A modern version of this is expressed in the phrase: 'There are two things that a child needs from their educators: roots and wings.' There is not one evil, there are two, and we must learn to find the path between such extremes through our moral intuition.

Since ancient times, evil has had a twofold aspect in many cultures. Homer writes about Scylla and Charybdis in *The Odyssey*. Scylla was a six-headed monster that snatched sailors from ships that sailed too close, but if they tried to avoid her, they risked being sucked down by Charybdis. In the Old Testament, we come across the two beasts Leviathan and Behemoth, the former rising up out of the sea, the latter approaching across the land (Job 40–41), and the New Testament speaks of the devil and Satan (Rev. 12:9). We recognise in these pairings the characteristics of Lucifer and Ahriman, two adversarial powers each pursuing their own goals.

What is Lucifer's goal? Lucifer wants to create a world in which everything runs on its own, where the human being is a marionette of God. Or in the language of our century: a moral robot, someone who does exactly what the spiritual world prescribes and keeps their hands clean on earth. Lucifer takes us into a world of illusion, of beauty and pretty appearance. And although, according to Steiner, Lucifer's rule ended during Christ's time on earth, we still flee out of the claws of Ahriman into his warm embrace – from one extreme into the other.

On the other hand, it is Ahriman's ideal to erase the past, and to live only in the here and now as a material robot, in a world of technology where all life is eventually eradicated. What in our time is happening on a large scale, the extermination of plant and animal species, is inspired by Ahriman. It used to be known that human beings consisted of body, soul and spirit. Since then, not only have we abolished the spirit, but we've also reduced the soul to a bundle of hormones and brain functions. Now Ahriman wants to crush the soul between the millstones of materialism.

One of Rudolf Steiner's verses begins with the lines: 'To spend oneself in matter / is to grind down souls.'[11] By this he meant that if we live long enough in the delusion of materialism, then we will eventually forfeit our immortality.

In the Offertory of the service of the Consecration of the Human Being we hear the prayer: '... that they bury not their eternal being for the sake of their temporal.' If we focus exclusively on the temporal all our life, we eventually lose the possibility of participating in eternal life. This is no poetic imagery, but a realistic possibility.

This brings us to one of the most troubling subjects in anthroposophy: the incarnation of Ahriman in our time. Despite giving nearly six thousand lectures in his lifetime, Steiner spoke of this on only seven occasions in lectures that he gave in 1919. According to him, early in the third millennium since Christ's advent, there will be 'an actual incarnation of Ahriman: Ahriman in the flesh'.[12] In these lectures, Steiner described a series of inevitable developments that are a preparation for Ahriman's future incarnation, and which, more than a hundred years after he gave these lectures, we can recognise everywhere around us:

- The spread of a mathematical, mechanistic view of the world
- Spiritual life will become fixed and lifeless, like information stored in libraries and now increasingly online
- The rise of nationalism
- The literal, materialistic interpretation of the gospels
- The development of clairvoyance without a corresponding moral development (we might think of the use of psychedelics here)
- Genetically manipulated food that estranges us from the spiritual world

To this point we have described the aims and ideals of the two great adversarial powers who oppose our future development. But Steiner also spoke about a third category of evil beings called the 'asuras'. The asuras will cause human beings to become possessed by their sexual instincts and caught up in black magic, the ultimate evil. According to Steiner, 'The black magician draws his most powerful forces out of the morass of sensuality. The purpose of sexual rites is to introduce such magic into these circles.'[13] Due to the workings of the asuras, parts of the human I will become irrevocably lost.

If we try to imagine the way the asuras work, and how we can thwart their activities with the help of Christ, it can be helpful to picture the Representative of Humanity. In this sculpture, Rudolf Steiner depicted Lucifer and Ahriman with Christ standing between them and holding the balance between the extremes. If Christ were to disappear, one can imagine the asuras would appear in this empty spot.

These days black magic is not an unknown phenomenon anymore. It is openly talked about and has found its way into popular music, modern art and the media.[14]

In 1993 an interview appeared in *Flensburger Hefte* with a representative of modern black magic. The interviewee's name was Ulla von Bernus, and she had been an active member of a Satanic church in Germany since she was sixteen. She had risen rapidly through the ranks, appearing regularly on German television in the 1980s and 1990s. But then, at the height of her career in the church, her life took an unexpected turn. Following the death of one of her acquaintances, the deceased soul appeared to her in a dream. The acquaintance led her through a dark passage that came out onto an open square bathed in a half-light. Suddenly, a rain of golden grain came down from above. In this heavenly gold Christ appeared and said to her: 'In the end, I am the victor.' This experience caused Ulla von Bernus, from one day to the next, to change sides from black magic to white. In this interview she relates how her life has changed since she immersed herself in white magic. She describes how the world of black magic is growing these days:

At this moment the adversarial powers have planet earth completely in their grip. People are fascinated by them. The powers of white magic give them the latitude to work to a certain extent, so of course the adversarial powers do that. Why are they not further restricted? People notice that and many follow them. It begins with black magic, but small stuff. From early morning to late at night people are flooded by the media, and most of what comes from the media is of a dubious nature. It is steered by Satan and his host, and absorbed by people subconsciously. They make people forget how to think clearly or concentrate; that is why there is now such a strong interest in dubious occult practices. Only a small number of people have the inclination to tread purely spiritual paths; most go for easier, grey options. From the moment I told my students that following a purely spiritual path is the only thing that counts, 90% of them fell away, because that is too difficult.[15]

Thus spoke someone with experience of how the adversarial forces in our time.

The suggestion that the adversarial forces have been given free play might seem like a good reason to be pessimistic about the future and could drive a person to despair. But we must resist this. As Steiner said, humanity cannot avoid this incarnation by Ahriman; it is something that has to happen. What is important, and what can give us confidence and courage in the face of this challenge, is if we can find the right attitude and approach to it. This is possible if we keep in mind that none of these adversarial powers is stronger than Christ, who in the end will triumph. During his life on earth, he was able to say, '…the prince of this world now stands condemned' (John 16:11).

However, overcoming the adversarial powers cannot ultimately be a matter of rejecting them, as though there is to be no place for them within the larger scheme of things. Rather, it must be a matter of recognising the necessity of their existence for the sake of evolution and consequently transforming them. In the spiritual stream of Manichaeism, we find an engagement with the powers of evil that builds on this fundamental insight. It is to this future-oriented spiritual stream that we turn in the following chapters.

11

Manichaeism and the Origins of Evil

Jesse Mulder

The subject of Manichaeism takes us back to early Christianity which, in the early centuries of its development and expansion, consisted of a rich and varied collection of streams and movements. Manichaeism was one of these streams – to be more precise, it was the largest of a number of gnostic streams within early Christianity. As used here the word *gnostic* indicates streams in which knowledge (Greek *gnosis*) of spiritual realities, mystery wisdom, was still preserved. The influential stream of Manichaeism had its origin in the dedication and commitment of its founder, Mani, who lived in the Middle East in the third century AD and undertook great journeys to spread his Christian-Gnostic movement and seek followers.

An important source on the life and teachings of Mani is the so-called Cologne Mani Codex, discovered in Upper Egypt in 1969 and believed to be written in the fourth or fifth century. The codex describes Mani as an exceptional human being who, at a decisive moment in his life, had an encounter with his so-called *syzygos*, his 'heavenly companion' – what we might think of as his higher I. From this heavenly companion, Mani learned about the secrets of humanity and the evolution of the world. He came to know human beings as beings possessing a divine inner core of goodness and light, but who have become ensnared in evil here in the darkness of the material world.

In what has ultimately been passed down to us as historical Manichaeism this theme of good and evil appears as a kind of eternal dualism. According to this interpretation, light and dark, good and evil, are both original. Besides God the Father, who reigns in the realm of light, there is an equally powerful ruler of darkness, meaning there will never be an end of evil.

In the only lecture he gave that was fully dedicated to Manichaeism, Rudolf Steiner said, 'If you come to know Manichaeism in this form it will seem radically un-Christian and quite incomprehensible.'[1] And indeed, you only need to read the beginning of the Prologue to the Gospel of John to realise this, for there it says: 'All things came into being through him, and nothing of all that has come into being was made except through him.' All things – including evil, therefore.

But we should of course not confuse this 'incomprehensible' interpretation with *original* Manichaeism. Before we now turn to real, 'practical' Manichaeism, it is useful to collect a number of elements that together can give us a picture of a 'true' Manichaean relationship to evil. For this I will first go back to a very big question, namely the *origin* of evil.

How evil came into being

In the chapter on the Apocalypse of St John it was indicated that we need to understand evil as something that is *allowed* by the good gods, because it is necessary for our development as free beings. In the lecture cycle *The Inner Realities of Evolution*, Rudolf Steiner gives a wonderful picture of the cosmic origin of evil. He sketches how in the very beginning of the creation a mighty offering was made by the Thrones, beings belonging to the highest angelic realm, the First Hierarchy. The Thrones looked up in ardent devotion to the spirits above them, the Cherubim, and to these Cherubim the Thrones offered the very substance of their being. It streamed out from them and became the substance out of which the physical world would eventually evolve. All physical substance, all matter, is an offering from the Thrones. A powerful thought!

But not all that was offered up by the Thrones was accepted by the Cherubim; they renounced a part of the offering. This was an extremely wise decision.

According to Steiner, the Cherubim are also called the Spirits of Harmony, a name that should be taken very literally. What appears as harmony in nature and world events consists of the deeds of these lofty, creative beings. They incorporated the offering from the Thrones into the harmony that they actually are – except for the part of the offering they rejected. This part was *not* made part of the great harmony of things.

Therefore, right at the beginning of the creation of the world, something came into being that is out of harmony with the rest, that holds things back, creates chaos and, yes, can even work destructively. The spiritual beings who then became entangled in this segregated part of the created substance became beings who would deviate from their original path of development. They became the opponents of the good gods.

As we know, a variety of adversarial powers have arisen during the great cosmic process of development. For this reason we spoke extensively in earlier chapters about the need for a demonology that provides clarity on the different powers and the way they work in humanity and the world. We mentioned Lucifer, the power that wants to let human beings revel in egoism and self-love, completely apart from the greater cosmic whole. We also spoke of Ahriman, the power that wants to turn human beings into cog wheels in a big, dead world machine. This is intended to represent an alternate reality, a rival of the cosmos of the good gods, just as Facebook now wants to develop the 'metaverse', a virtual, three-dimensional real-time world that is better than the real one. And we mentioned the asuras, an adversarial power that aims for total destruction and perversion and wants to entrap human beings in black magic.

The existence of these adversarial forces, which, each in its own way, oppose the great cosmic whole, can therefore be traced back to the Cherubim's deed of resignation we just described. This is not to say that the Cherubim created the adversarial powers themselves, but rather that through their resignation, their renunciation of the offering of the Thrones, they *allowed* these powers to come into being.

As a result of this, there arose on a cosmic scale the great opposition of light and darkness that Mani described. But as we have learned, human beings are the focus of these great cosmic developments. Each one of us is a 'little world', a microcosm in the macrocosm. We bear both light and darkness, good and evil within us. In Chapter 9, in which I discussed morality as a creative principle, I tried to describe a concrete example of this, namely the forces of destruction that exist within us and that are able to destroy matter. We owe it to this dark element within us that we have become autonomous beings. We are not simply part of the great harmony of things but have had to find our place in it *on our own*. It is up to us to find one of the twelve roads to the New Jerusalem.

The fact that we stand at this crucial crossing point of free will is directly connected with the history of the Cherubim, who in the primal beginning let an aspect of the world come into being that fell out of harmony with the great cosmic world. This part has been woven not just into our own being, but also into the world. That is why the earth is the place where, in freedom, we must undertake our task of encountering with evil, and out of freedom unfold our morality, our own creative forces.

The Manichaean relationship to evil

There is an extremely profound Manichaean legend with which we can connect this cosmic perspective of the origin of evil. This legend describes how the beings of darkness attempted to conquer the light realm, but when they came to the boundaries of the light realm they were repelled and their attack failed. They had to be punished, but –

and this is the extremely profound, deeply Manichaean aspect of this legend – in the light realm nothing evil existed, for only the good reigns there. Nothing could be found with which to punish the beings of darkness. What to do?

The beings of light then took part of themselves, light particles, and mingled these particles with the world of darkness. Once such parts of the light realm became mixed with the realm of darkness, they began to work like a kind of leaven. This created great turmoil in the dark realm with the result that a new element came into being: death. Since then, the realm of darkness has always carried the seed of its own destruction within itself.

The amazing aspect of this legend is that *we human beings* are that part of the light realm that was implanted into the realm of darkness. This is the Manichaean picture of the human being. We are the inhabitants of the realm of darkness, the material world, who carry such light particles within ourselves. We are the ones who must find a way to vanquish the realm of darkness, not through battle, but by leading it through its own death.

In this profound legend we find the distinctive element of the spiritual stream of Manichaeism beautifully expressed, namely that evil cannot be vanquished through battle, neither through exclusion nor punishment, but only by approaching it with mildness and love: an offering of an element of the light realm. The essential characteristic of Manichaeism is that it does not want to defend itself against evil, rather it wants to bring light into the innermost being of evil. Evil is thus not *fought* from outside but *redeemed* from within.

When we contemplate this Manichaean relationship to evil, we ultimately see that this is the *only* way to arrive at a solution to the problem of evil. Evil was *allowed* by the Cherubim, the Spirits of Harmony, who by their resignation, by not accepting part of the offering of the Thrones, created a space within which certain spiritual beings were able to oppose them. But these beings were not originally adversaries, of course. They, too, were bearers of the harmony that is administered by the Cherubim. Therefore, ever since these beings remained behind in their evolution and became adversaries, the great cosmic whole has been missing part of itself. It is therefore of essential importance for the fulfilment of cosmic evolution that these adversarial powers are eventually redeemed.

A familiar example: rights and duties

This cosmic perspective of the origin and redemption of the adversarial forces is so big and extensive that it is difficult to connect it with our everyday human experience. It would also be presumptuous to think that in our age we can definitively redeem these adversarial powers. It is questionable as to whether we are even capable of developing the mildness and love needed to take us in that direction. Evil consists of many forms, and it is better to stay far away from some of them until we have acquired the necessary inner strength and purity to face them without becoming overwhelmed. The 'key of David', which was mentioned in the chapter on the Apocalypse, will play an essential role in this process.

This explains why Rudolf Steiner indicates that Manichaeism is mostly a future stream. It has an important task to undertake much later in our human development; in our own time it is working more in the background in a preparatory way.

However, this does not mean that we must not, nor cannot, do anything with it. Let us look at an example that connects with the theme of our moral development. Morally speaking, the two adversarial powers we have to deal with most of all are Lucifer and Ahriman. We can understand this if we look at the concepts of *rights* and *duties*. Rights have something luciferic in them: what I consider as my right obviously has something of the nature of self-love, egocentricity, in it. I can easily embrace my rights, because after all, they are *my* rights! On the other hand, duties have something ahrimanic in them: I simply have to do them. Duties always have something cold and impersonal about them; they are part of the objective progression of world events.

Imagine, on the one hand, someone who revels in demanding everything that is their right and, on the other, someone who dutifully follows all manner of protocols and regulations. Especially in the turbulent time of COVID-19, both of these one-sided attitudes became extremely pronounced, both in people who dutifully obeyed the safety measures to the letter, and in people who got worked up about their rights being violated.

Rights are thus connected with a luciferic one-sidedness of subjective self-love, and duties with an ahrimanic one-sidedness of an objective, impersonal, even inhuman nature. These two face each other, and we can only overcome them if in dealing with each one we make use of the opposing power. If we apply to our duties the self-love of Lucifer, and thus learn to connect our duties more with ourselves and view them as *our own* duties so that we can then *love* them, then we overcome the cold, mechanical, impersonal nature of these duties. In doing so we contribute to the redemption of Lucifer's own entrapment by self-love. We give Lucifer a place in world events that is more in accord with the greater harmony.

And if, on the other hand, we view our rights with a certain *resignation*, a willingness to accept our place in world events and our part of world karma, then we bring something of Ahriman's coolness into our relationship to our rights. We thus contribute to the redemption of Ahriman by giving part of his being a place in the world that also fits in with the great harmony.

In this way, we can now take the first steps in the direction of the redemption of the adversarial powers. But, as Bastiaan Baan shows in the next chapter, this example of the moral aspects of rights and duties is only one of many possibilities for such steps.

The Last Judgment

After this brief excursion, let us turn again to the task of Manichaeism for the future of the earth. Our current time, as mentioned repeatedly before, stands under the sign of freedom, and is therefore connected with our struggle with evil – for these two, freedom and evil, are connected. It is an open question for each of us individually as to where this struggle will lead us. For this is the essential nature of our freedom, that it is *possible* to choose both good and evil. And we owe it precisely to the existence of the adversarial powers that this possibility exists.

But as it says in the Gospel of John, 'A time is coming and in fact has come' (John 16:32). We do not have an infinite amount of time at our disposal to engage in this struggle. A moment will come when a final outcome will have to be determined, namely when our current earth existence comes to an end. Then it will depend on our deeds whether we can be saved from what in the Creed of The Christian Community is called 'the death of matter'. A part of humanity will be able to develop themselves to that point, another part will not. There will be people who connect with evil with heart and soul. Yes, the dark pages of twentieth-century history, of the terrors of world wars, death camps and concentration camps, clearly show that this is no illusion.

But as long as our time on earth still lasts, it will always be possible *for everyone* to come to themselves and make a decisive turn. And that is when Manichaeism will play a crucial role. In that future decisive time, the Manichaeans will be those who do not close themselves off from people who have become entrapped in evil, but are able to connect with them. Precisely this will be the task of Manichaeans towards the decisive, final age of our earth: to make this turnabout possible through love and devotion.

12

Manichaeism and the Redemption of Evil

In the Lord's Prayer we find the petition: 'Deliver us from evil,' Whereas Manichaeism asks: 'Help us to redeem evil.' We know from experience that both will take a long time. We usually have the deeply rooted desire to restrain evil and, if possible, eliminate it. And the tendency to wash our hands of evil has even deeper roots.

Ever since President George W. Bush called a number of countries the 'axis of evil', countless politicians have used this term to scapegoat others while keeping their own hands clean. That tendency is not limited to politicians. If we look honestly at ourselves, we find that we all have this tendency to blame and demonise others. Our instinctive reaction to evil is annoyance, irritation, anger and the inclination to eradicate it. But evil is a dragon with many heads. When you cut one of them off, two will take its place. The Jewish Rabbi Naftali used to say: 'I have tried to break the evil tendency, but when I did that I had two evil tendencies.'[1]

While for most of us the redemption of evil is a task that lies in the far distant future, it is already a reality for initiates. This is why in the occult tradition they are called the Masters of Wisdom and Harmony of Feelings. In a notebook from the year 1906, Rudolf Steiner wrote about them:

The Masters are no bastion against evil, but the leaders in absorbing evil. We must not isolate evil but rather include it and use it in service of the good. The rage of a lion remains a form of evil as long as it is used in an egoistic manner. If someone would use this rage to perform a service to a fellow human being, its force would work for the good. Evil is not real. Evil is misplaced good. Only with this knowledge is spiritual alchemy possible.[2]

Alchemy is the transformation of the material world, the transubstantiation of matter. It will be possible for us in the distant future – as it is for initiates here and now – to transubstantiate evil.

Someone who could speak about this from his own experience was Mahatma Gandhi, who wrote:

I have learned through bitter experience the one supreme lesson to conserve my anger, and as heat conserved is transmuted into energy, even so our anger can be transmuted into a power which can move the world.[3]

If you restrain the force that wants to express itself in anger and put it in the service of another person, you are transubstantiating evil. This is not something we are able to do on our own; we have to be in the company of helping powers that have already reached the goal of transforming evil.

In his book *Nacht und Nebel* (Night and Fog), Floris Bakels describes such a moment in a confrontation with the camp commander of an infamous concentration camp. Together with a large group of inmates he had to work in a quarry. He had to throw stones into a dump truck with a shovel. He was the first on the scene and took a small shovel to conserve energy.

My back began to sting, my arms were failing, my knees were buckling ... then I felt the shovel was yanked out of my hands, and I smelled sweat and perfume: the monster Ernst Jager was standing next to me. He produced a beautiful new shovel, a big one, and said, very softly, almost politely: 'And now I will teach you to work.'

Then the guard turned away. When he came back the next day, Floris Bakels expected the torment to continue. But as he walked up to the quarry, he heard a voice say: 'Be not afraid of those who can kill the body but cannot kill the soul. Why are you so afraid? Have you no faith?' At the quarry the camp commander came over to him:

With him approached Jesus Christ. The thought came to me: what can this man do to me? What can he do against God, his Creator? This is a human being like me, only unfortunately possessed by the devil ... I must not fear; I must pray for his release. I stopped work and waited. The thousand quarry workers also stopped work and watched. Jager stood before me and bawled something: 'You have to load the truck!' What I then said I have never been able to remember, but it was something like: 'It is not good that you treat me like an enemy. We are all in the same boat. We have to help each other. You know that I can't handle this work. You are not in the world to beat me to death, but to help me.' That was the beginning of an hour-long discussion. Jager displayed an almost bestial stupidity. Among other things, he interrogated me about the word 'friend'. What was that, a 'friend'? After an hour we shook hands ... he never bothered me anymore. Whoever calls this proof of superhuman bravery is under an illusion. Rather, it is an eloquent example of the power God grants someone in despair, someone who believes in him and asks him for help. The angels had been standing around me.[4]

Floris Bakels was helped in inhuman circumstances by a superhuman power. It can often look as though we are all alone, but perhaps that is not entirely true. What does the voice of conscience say face to face with evil?

A contemporary of Floris Bakels was in a Japanese concentration camp during the Second World War. When confronting evil he experienced the human measure of the speaking conscience. One of the officers of the camp ordered a roll call of the inmates. One by one they had to step forward to be beaten with a stick. After receiving this treatment and walking back, he saw that his neighbour hardly had the strength to stand. He wouldn't survive this beating. Then sounded an inner voice that told him: 'Go again.' He stepped forward and looked the officer in the eye. The latter was completely confused because the same inmate appeared before him again. He dropped his stick and walked away. The rage of the officer disappeared as if by magic and was replaced by impotence. Yes, the conscience of the inmate spoke clearly, but the inmate himself had to take the initiative to perform the deed.

Conscience does not always speak so clearly. But we also know that evil cannot be vanquished with violence. On the contrary, things go from bad to worse. From time to time the world is on fire because we are throwing oil on the flames. Only by self-discipline and holding back can evil be warded off in the right way. Even in wars – if they follow the rules of the art – this is a maxim: respond to the violence of the enemy in proportion, not with revengeful actions that provoke even more violence. In Germany this is called *Konfliktfähigkeit*, the ability to handle conflicts. Sometimes this capacity consists only of the art of remaining silent when others are slandering.

This is what Ita Wegman did when she faced unjust criticism from leading anthroposophists in the 1930s. When a group of students visited her, one of them asked: 'Why don't you reply to all those accusations? Why don't you do something?' Her answer was: 'One should not feed the demons, but starve them.' By not defending herself against the allegations, but by ignoring them, she did not give her opponents the chance to escalate the conflict.[5]

That is how Manichaeism works, by transforming evil through mildness. Rudolf Steiner said in a lecture on November 11, 1904: '[Future humanity] will have the task of drawing evil back into the continuing stream of evolution through kindness.' He was not speaking here about the ultimate redemption of evil, but about a gradual transformation. He continued:

> Then a spiritual current will be born which does not oppose
> evil, even though it manifests in the world in its demonic form
> ... evil must be included again in evolution and be overcome,
> not by strife, but only through charitableness. It is the task of
> the Manichaean spiritual stream forcefully to prepare for this.[6]

This careful formulation clearly shows that for the time being there is still a long way to go. What is being prepared through Manichaeism will be tried and tested to the extreme as our times grow more demonic. In spite of this we must still ask ourselves: 'What do we do when confronted with evil?' Although I suspect that real Manichaeans can today only be found like needles in a haystack, even with our own limited capacities we can look for answers to all our daily trials. We can get a sense of how this can be achieved when we consider the words of St Paul: 'I speak the truth in Christ – I am not lying, my conscience confirms it through the Holy Spirit' (Rom. 9:1).

Rudolf Steiner occasionally spoke of developing a more sensitive conscience.[7] We can practise this if we consult our conscience before a particular action and also afterwards. Both in anticipation and in review, conscience has things to say that can serve us as an inner compass.

Thinking back to the chapter on ancient forms of prophecy, we might consider that in our modern time, the ability to see into the future lies in our conscience. Conscience is my prophet – provided I make it sufficiently sensitive. Indeed, in a few exceptional cases, people have told me that before a deed they imaginatively foresaw the consequences of this deed.

I once visited a man who, after a heart attack, had ended up in a hospital. He was in a conflict with a colleague in which he had fought his opponent by any means, and dragged his colleague's name through the mud in an effort to get the better of him. One night he had a vivid dream in which he saw the door to his house opening. His enemy stood before him and made a fervent gesture: 'Stop!' Although this dream contained a serious warning, the man continued his slander campaign. It ended abruptly with a heart attack and a long period of unemployment. Afterwards, the man had the feeling that he had been perfidious – and not only towards his colleague. With wilful malice he had denied even the voice of his conscience.

When sensitising our conscience we should also practise a particular form of review. A variation on the well-known adage 'If you want to improve the world, start with yourself', might be 'If you want to redeem evil, start with yourself'. This requires that we get to know the dark side of our personality, our dark twin brother or sister. The psychiatrist Carl Jung called it the Shadow.

Most people don't care to know that they have this double, let alone possess the inclination to get to know it. However, in extraordinary cases, such as shortly before dying, people meet their double as a real being that has been connected with them their entire life. A colleague who was lying on his deathbed said one day before his passing: 'Last night I saw my dark twin brother. But that was not nice...' It is known that terminal patients before their death often experience a surge of energy. Experienced nurses and doctors know that this can be a sign of approaching death.[8]

Rudolf Steiner describes the double as an unredeemed being that enters us shortly before birth and leaves just before death. In our next incarnation this being confronts us with the consequences of our aberrations, denials and weaknesses – in brief, with the balance of our karma.

Sculptor Doorlie Gerdes depicted this being in a sculpture called The Double. It shows a human being bent over, burdened by his own image that lies along his back. It is an inextricable part of himself. We discover our double by exploring the unknown side of our personality, for instance, by learning to understand the language of our dreams.

Figure: 12.1: The Double. Bronze sculpture by Doorlie Gerdes (1973).

Frequently our dream life at night has comments on our conscious day life, albeit in enigmatic, sometimes obscure pictures. For more than fifty years I have kept a dream diary. By systematically writing my dreams down and comparing them, I was, from time to time, able to understand what the double wanted to tell me. After I had been following my double intensively for a year, I wrote the following poem:

I'm going bent and crooked
With burdens that have lifelong been
Assigned to me.
There is no light, no countenance.
Only a voice
Accosting me:
I will not let you go.

I ask, I seek,
I plead, I curse.
I want to be no slave
Of my dark likeness.
But he says quite unmoved,
Without commiseration:
I will not let you go.

Then he is watching me,
His gaze is blurred
As in a cloudy sky
From which falls endless rain.
And suddenly,
As if the clouds tear open,
He calls to me:
I will not let you go –
Unless you bless me.

Just as in Jacob's struggle with the angel, this dark angel, this double, can also give its blessing to whoever struggles with it openly. In Chapter 9, Jesse Mulder referred to the Manichaean legend that relates how, when the Spirits of Darkness attacked the Realm of Light, the Spirits of Light sent part of their world into the Realm of Darkness in the form of light particles.

In other words, just as the core of evil has its origin in the good – which after all is the origin of everything that has ever been created – so evil also has a germ of the good in it. Through the help of the Spirits of Light, we human beings can redeem evil. The best summary of this challenge facing the practical Manichaeism of the future is expressed in a poem by Christian Morgenstern that ends with the words:

Brother be to all!
Help and service give to all!
Is, since He appeared,
Goal alone!

Even the evil-doers
Who oppose advance!
Once they too were fashioned forth
From the light.

Love the evil – good!
So deep souls direct.
Learn by hate to reinforce –
Valiant love!

Brothers, hear the word!
Let it grow to truth –
So our earth will one day be
God's own Home![9]

13

Current Trends and Developments

I want you to panic. I want you to feel the fear I feel every day.
And then I want you to act. I want you to act as you would in a crisis.
I want you to act as if your house is on fire. Because it is.

Greta Thunberg

In February 2022 there appeared a report from the United Nations with the conclusion that the goals of the climate agreement reached in Paris in 2015 will not be reached by a long shot. In this study it was stated that countries worldwide want to extract more fossil fuels – yes, twice the amounts of oil, gas and coal as stated in the original Paris Agreement. This means that the goal of the agreement – an increase in the temperature of the earth in 2040 of not more than 1.5°C (2.7°F) – has been exceeded. UN Secretary General Antonio Guterres spoke in his commentary of 'failing climate leadership' of the responsible politicians and organisations, and of the great polluters 'that were guilty of setting fires in our only house'.

The outcome of the report inevitably means that all kinds of goals reached in the original climate agreement are up in the air again. The new prognosis – which no doubt will have to be revised again in the future – is that in one hundred years the average temperature will have risen by 3°C if we keep producing and consuming on the current scale. These kinds of developments only increase the feeling of urgency on the part of many people and organisations.

For example, Extinction Rebellion, a group that is sounding the alarm on every continent, uses non-violent civil disobedience to demand climate justice and a rapid transition to a fossil-free industry. They are facing not only the established order and the power of industry and politics, but also the lethargy and indifference of a large part of the population. Norwegian anthropologist Thor Heyerdal said about this: 'People think that if they let the pipelines for the discharge of their sewer systems run far enough away from the beach into the sea, the waste will, so to say, fall off the edge of the world.'[1]

Even if we don't care about it at all, the idea of the 'end of times' holds a fascinating appeal for many people today. It is a theme with which millions are made in films and games, and of course it is a mainstay in the teaching of many churches. Fundamentalist groups preach the approaching downfall of the world and even use their shortsighted prophecies to proclaim that it is an exercise in futility to try and save the climate. On the contrary, Christian fundamentalism looks for the Second Coming of Christ, not a way to reform the world.

Across the Christian world there is a movement called Prosperity Theology.[2] This movement teaches that the Bible has promised prosperity to the faithful, and that by simply expressing one's wish and believing that God will fulfil it, then the wish is granted. Because the end of the world is near, it is completely superfluous to worry about the environment, the climate crisis, injustice and poverty in the world, for: 'Jesus comes, praise Jesus!' All we need to do is preach the gospel (and by this is meant the gospel of wealth, the prosperity gospel) and wait for the approaching end of the world.

This feeling of urgency does not only live in activists and Christian fundamentalists – which of course have very different objectives – but also in science. The Stockholm Resilience Institute, which studies trends for the future, regularly publishes its *Planetary Boundaries* report in which scientists outline developments in the areas of climate and the environment. One of the disturbing developments the report has identified is the fivefold increase in the production of chemicals since 1950. Around 350,000 different chemicals are manufactured today, and the expectation is that this figure will rise to three times as many by the year 2050. Between 2000 and 2015 the production of plastics alone has increased by 75%. Plastics contain more than 10,000 different chemicals. Most people have no idea what impact the combination of these substances has on the environment. More worrying still, the global water cycle is showing new disturbances, and virtually everywhere on earth moisture in the soil is drying up.[3]

A generally used indication of the state of the world is the so-called ecological footprint. With approximately 7.5 billion people living on earth, our consumption of the planet's resources is 1.5 times greater than it can produce. We are living far beyond our means. We are in all respects committing predatory exploitation. And if we all consumed the same amount as the residents of the U.S.A., we would need the resources of five earths.

Here I would like to cast a different light on this depressing perspective of the exploitation of our earth. This involves correcting, or at least revising, the usual story of our planet, which says that the earth's best days are behind it and that it is in decline, accelerated by what human beings are doing. 'The dying earth existence', a formula from the Creed of The Christian Community, seems to be an inescapable reality. The only thing that sooner or later is certain for the physical world is death. This is also an incontestable law in physics. When all energy has been converted into warmth, not only the earth but the whole cosmos will succumb to heat death, to entropy. Although doubts have been raised in new theories of physics regarding this form of dying, still the end result is the same. People then imagine that through the expansion of the universe a 'big chill', not heat, will lead to death. Such are the usual ideas about the dying earth.

Buzz Holling, a prominent ecologist and leader in his profession, developed the theory of 'panarchy' based on the observation of living nature (from the Greek *pan*, which means 'all', 'everything', and is also the name given to the god of nature; and *archē*, meaning 'dominion', 'reign'). Everywhere in nature he recognised the same law. Systems in nature are not static but dynamic. Everywhere they follow a certain pattern that takes its course in four phases:

- Phase 1: Growth, upbuilding, accumulation, flexibility.
- Phase 2: Conservation, consolidation. This means that natural sources are no longer available for growth and expansion; the natural system loses its original flexibility.
- Phase 3: The old, rigidified structure degenerates and is destroyed.
- Phase 4: Reorganisation, renewal – new entities enter the system.

In simple terms: panarchy is the interaction between life and death. The same goes for all life on earth. Not only in ecology, but in all social, economic and legal systems the same goes on: the development of a new initiative begins a phase of growth and consolidation, which is then followed sooner or later by a declining phase that leads to death. According to Buzz Holling, this holds true not only for individual systems, but also for the world system as a whole. In his own words: 'Some kind of systemic breakdown is almost certain now.'[4]

Holling's model shows resilience to some extent, but also that this resilience is finite when a system is put under structural pressure for a long time. Indeed, our entire earth is going through a dying process, but that does not mean an irrevocable death. Nature and culture show us that death is the condition for new life. In the words of Goethe: 'Life is the most beautiful invention of nature, and death is the trick of nature to have much life.'[5]

The theory of panarchy can be illustrated by the following diagram:

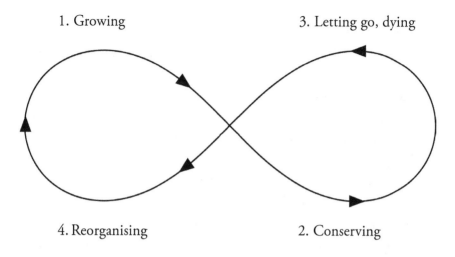

1. Growing   3. Letting go, dying

4. Reorganising   2. Conserving

Figure 13.1: Diagram showing how systems develop in ecology.

In the past ten years of my life, I have worked intensively with the subject of the future of the earth. By the fact alone of living with the question 'Is there a future for the earth?', my perspective of the future has been enlarged. To write this book I retired for a month into a little house in the wilds of Sweden, hidden in a hamlet of ten houses. Not only did this isolation create the possibility to focus on this one theme; it also made it possible to look from a distance at the world around me. I had not forgotten the dismal state of the world, and yet, surrounded by nature, I was aware that life goes on, even when people threaten each other as well as nature. Panarchy, the God of nature, has the last word. This does not mean that we don't need to worry, on the contrary.

Let us go back to the latest developments. Of the countless alarming reports published by the organisation World Watch (a predecessor of the Stockholm Resilience Institute), I want to shed some more light on one of them. Until 2017, State of the World regularly published flood maps showing those areas of the world that are threatened with flooding. Worldwide almost all coasts on every continent are in danger.

Ten percent of the world population lives near the sea; this includes millions of people who already experience flooding from time to time. Think of Bangladesh, New Orleans, and even New York. The greatest danger for the future of this city is flooding. But the entire east coast of North and South America is in danger, where the consequences of the rising sea level are made more severe because the land is also sinking. On the west coast of America, the effects are less extreme.

Geophysicists who study the rising sea level speak of 'a gradual Atlantis': slowly but surely America is being submerged. A child born in our time may, as an adult, witness a 6-foot sea-level rise. That is the prognosis if the average temperature on earth increases by 1.5°C – but the latest prognoses go higher than 1.5°C, meaning that there could be more than a 6-foot sea-level rise.

Until recently people in western Europe spoke of 'the storm of the century', a combination of a spring tide and a strong northwestern wind by which the Gulfstream in the Atlantic is whipped up. It has been concluded that these days we cannot speak of the storm of the century anymore, for several such storms have already taken place. Towards the year 2050 the risk of such weather conditions will be five times as great as it used to be. It has been calculated that a 2°C increase in the temperature of the earth will cause a sea level rise of close to 15 feet. World Watch mentions the possibility of a 3°C increase. In that case, most of Manhattan will be under water.

To many people, these prognoses sound like theory or fantasy, but in the meantime all kinds of measures are taken to keep the water out of the city. The possibility has been studied to protect New York with locks, like the ones used in The Netherlands. Dutch water engineers have been consulted for this. The city of New York, with all its islands and curving coastlines, has a coast of over 500 miles. It proves to be impossible to protect all of that from water incursion. The only thing that is now being considered is the plan to build a wall around Wall Street, so that the richest part of the city will be preserved as an island. For most New Yorkers this perspective does not yet play a role in their lives, although large parts of the city were inundated by Hurricane Sandy in 2012. Currently, bad storms will cause flooding in the subways and airports. Every day 13 million gallons (57.2 million litres) of water have to be pumped out of the subways to allow the trains to run.

The ones who are really concerned and are taking measures are the real estate and insurance companies. The insurance company Swiss Re has already calculated that towards 2050 the losses of industry in New York will be $4.5 billion (£3.5 billion) per year. Based on this prognosis insurance premiums have been raised accordingly. Real estate company Zillow, Inc. calculates that towards 2050 two million homes will have to be given up. The same goes for factories, tunnels and other infrastructure.

This is the example of the huge consequences for one city of millions, but it applies to the entire east coast of America. We remember New Orleans, of which two thirds was flooded by Hurricane Katrina in 2005. And this will happen not only in America, but to billions of people all over the world.

In The Netherlands, due to our experience of floods and inundations, we have become a little wiser than the rest of the world when it comes to flood management. Dutch engineers are often consulted in problem areas all over the world. In the course of time, however, they have learned that it is better to make space for the water than to build dams, dikes and locks. Thanks to the project Space for the River, which created large flood plains along rivers, the damage of floods could be somewhat mitigated in that country.

Besides the mounting ecological crisis, there is another development that is just as alarming. I am referring to what is called the 'infocalypse'. Not only is there is an apocalypse relating to world events, but there is also one involving the spread of information and our ability to distinguish truth from lies. So called deep-fake technology makes it increasingly difficult to tell real pictures and videos from those that have been artificially created, and the rapid evolution of artificial intelligence will impact all areas of social life.[6] Things have already become so difficult that politicians such as Joe Biden and Emmanuel Macron employ experts whose task it is to unmask disinformation.

The plans to create a 'metaverse' (from the Greek *meta*, meaning 'beyond', and Latin *universum*, meaning 'universe': beyond the universe) have already partly been realised in 'metaverse companies' offering various products and services. In 2021 Meta Platforms, Inc. was founded by Facebook-creator Mark Zuckerberg, which combined Facebook, WhatsApp, Instagram and other social media platforms for the purpose of creating a virtual reality. The term 'metaverse' comes from the 1992 science-fiction novel *Snow Crash* by Neal Stephenson. In it he describes a fictitious computer-world where the principal characters lead a second life. So alluring and deceptive is this world that they ultimately decide to stay connected with the metaverse for good. In his statement *The Metaverse and How We'll Build It Together*, Zuckerberg presented his vision of the leading role the metaverse will play in our society (though some might call it a *mis*leading role).[7] Since then, much that he described has been realised.

The relentless pace of these developments is alarming, especially when so little time seems to be given to considering the impacts they could have on humanity. Kevin Kelley, one of the founders of *Wired* magazine, which looks at the effects emerging technology has on culture, wrote a kind of evolutionary theory of technical developments in which he concluded: 'The technological development of which we are part has a will of its own, which no one can stop. All we can do is embrace it.'[8] What we are used to regarding as an objective, technological world has a will of its own.

From an anthroposophical perspective we could say that a spiritual being is at work in the background. Indeed, behind every physical phenomenon a spiritual being is working. This is not only true for all living things, but also for un-ensouled nature – the realm of the elements and elemental beings. In the case of the material world, the world of machines, electricity and magnetism, this being is Ahriman.

That does not mean that this world is bad; rather, it depends on how we use technology. When technology is used to spread disinformation on a large scale, the way this is being done these days in 'troll factories', it is evident that demons are at work.

This is the theme of the Apocalypse: in the foreground there are active persons who bring about good or evil, while behind them stand spiritual powers who inspire them and wage the battle for the human soul. And we are the battlefield. This ongoing battle causes an irrevocable separation between spirits. The Apocalypse shows how humanity breaks up into a part that tries to live in the truth and another part that lives in the lie. This break culminates in the imagination of Babylon and the New Jerusalem (Rev. 18–21).

We can see the beginning of this trend already in our own time. Social media companies have facilitated the spread of misinformation and conspiracy theories that are having a damaging effect on our societies. It used to be said that in political debates, for example, people agreed on what the facts were, they just disagreed on their significance or on what they meant. But in our post-truth world it seems as though we cannot even agree on what the facts are. People promote 'alternative facts', and the choice in elections increasingly seems to be between, not two different views of the same reality, but of two entirely different realities.[9]

All the old forms of social, economic and political life appear doomed, but often out of catastrophe there arises something no one expected. The classic expression of courage in the face of despair is Pandora's box, a 'gift' from Zeus to humanity as retribution for Prometheus stealing fire from heaven and giving it to human beings. When the box was opened all the misery of the world poured out. The only thing that was left was hope. Courage in the face of despair is a realistic hope. There is a reason not to be desperate, even when we lose the ground under our feet. For under the abyss is the primal ground, the divine world, which bears the unbearable and brings order into chaos.

For this reason, we must always keep in mind that, while in the physical world we have a tendency to focus on results, the spiritual world does things differently. It does not regard physical results, but instead considers moral intentions. It does not count, it weighs. This is an age-old image that continues to be relevant today. In the Egyptian Book of the Dead, Osiris weighs the dead, and in near-death experiences of the twentieth and twenty-first centuries we hear again and again that the spiritual world weighs the moral value of the human being.

Friedrich Rittelmeyer once experienced an eloquent expression of this in a dream about a deceased person. During his life this man was a highly respected person, well-to-do, influential, authoritative, a 'weighty' personality. A few weeks after his passing, the deceased appeared to Rittelmeyer in a dream, as lean as a rake, and said: 'This is all that is left of me.' Nothing to do with outer appearance and fame counts with the spiritual world.

I would like to end this chapter with the experiences of a cultural pessimist and a cultural optimist, both of whom regard the future in their own individual way: Yuval Noah Harari and Heinrich Ogilvie.

Harari belongs to the outstanding materialists of the twenty-first century. He subscribes to the world view that everything in evolution is the result of coincidence, and that the human being is an accidental product of genetically determined factors. How did *homo sapiens* come into being? According to Harari:

Accidental gene mutations created new cable connections in the brain of *homo erectus*. As a result he could think in a completely new way and communicate through new forms of language. As far as we could judge this, it was pure coincidence.[10]

This is how Harari describes the accidental product *homo sapiens* in his book *Homo Deus*. He does not accept the idea that human beings have a task that lifts them above their natural state, and which was given to them in Genesis: 'fill the earth and subdue it' (Gen. 1:28).

Indeed, this verse has all too frequently been misused even today, to torture and exploit nature and our fellow human beings. However, the Hebrew expression used in Genesis has a different meaning. The expression that is usually translated as 'subdue it' means literally: bring it [the earth] under the feet. Human beings have the task of walking on the whole earth, to get to know it, and to humanise it. Also the assignment to 'have dominion over the fish of the sea and over the birds of the air and over every living thing that moves upon the earth' (Gen. 1:28) has been one-sidedly translated. At the time when the Old Testament was written down, the Hebrew word for reigning (in the Revised Standard Version rendered as 'having dominion over') also had the meaning of *caring for*. Human beings receive the task to acquire insight and oversight over the realm of the animals, and to care for it.[11]

By contrast, Harari describes the task of the human being in culture, religion and humanism as genetically mis-programmed brain development. At one time during their development, human beings became *homo erectus*, 'upright man'. Subsequently, in the course of evolution they became *homo sapiens*, the 'wise human', but we have the task, says Harari, to become *homo deus*, to become gods. He imagines a future of 'bodies, brains and minds', the principal product of the twenty-first century. The body will be instrumentalised and augmented by technology, and brains will be improved with the aid of computer programs, so that our intelligence will make a leap in evolution. Harari calls that the marriage with machines. He realises what the consequence will be:

Democracy and the free market will collapse as soon as Google and Facebook will know us better than we know ourselves. Authority will no longer be in the hands of individual people, but of algorithms and networks.[12]

Homo deus has the future destiny of being upgraded through biological manipulation, by the implanting of chips, and by changes in DNA. This is not future fantasy because these things are practised in laboratories today. For example, research is being conducted into nanobots, microscopic robots, that can be implanted into the bloodstream and help to regulate our health and fight disease.[13] Harari does not resist this, rather he embraces the technological development and describes a future world in which the reality of the spirit is completely absent. At the same time, in his daily life, he practises a form of Buddhism called vipassana meditation. The aim of this meditation is to let go of all attachment and all forms of suffering and happiness. For him, meditation is not a way to know the spiritual world, but, away from religion and the philosophy of life, to distance oneself from the illusion of the independently thinking individual and the illusions of the world.

In contrast to this is the perspective of an optimist who lived with the reality of the spiritual world. That is how Heinrich Ogilvie, one of the founders of The Christian Community, appeared to me.

Shortly before his death, Ogilvie gave an interview in which he gave his vision of the future.[14] Ever since the foundation of The Christian Community he lived with the ideal of what he called 'the all-encompassing cultural revolution'. That ideal turned out to be an illusion; the cultural revolution, as he imagined it, did not take place. The interviewer asked him how he viewed the near future, and Ogilvie gave a remarkable answer: 'I had hoped that during my life the actual change, the revolution, would take place. Our last hope is that change will come as a result of catastrophe, when it does not happen out of free will.'

The reporter was confused. 'That means chaos – or do you imagine a form of terrorism?'

Ogilvie replied: 'The catastrophe does not bring good will by itself, but as a result of the catastrophe hearts and heads will open a bit.

After that, something has to come into them.'

'To many people it does not look like a regular catastrophe,' the reporter said. 'The next catastrophe might well be the definitive one, might be the last.'

Ogilvie replied: 'But that is exactly what gives me hope: that the impulse of Christ, which is hidden in the hearts of people, will make it possible that in the downfall of our culture a new ascent becomes possible.'

Ogilvie knew what he was talking about. He had been on the front lines in two world wars. He had been on the battlefield, he had been wounded, and he had seen many die. In the catastrophes of the world wars, he had seen how new life had arisen out of death, out of the downfall.

14.

What Can I Do?

I think that we draw the most intense and important form
of hope from the supersensory, the only form of hope which,
in spite of everything, can keep us on our feet and
encourage us to good deeds.

Vaclav Havel

Conscience is God's substitute on earth.

Novalis

Caring for the earth is a moral and religious task, one that our Creator gave to us at the very beginning of our development. Francis of Assisi was the living example of this religious dimension of caring for the earth. In his *Cantico del frate Sole* he sings of brother sun, sister moon, mother earth, sister water, sister light. All creatures receive their rightful place in service to the divine world. This is no vague pantheism, but divine service in the sense of the well-known words from the Gospel of Matthew: 'What you have done to the least of my brethren you have done to me.'

Because it is our responsibility as human beings to care for the earth, we must act first before our heavenly helpers can come to our aid. The fact that the angels are powerless without the initiative of human beings is impressively portrayed in a work of art that came into being in an exceptional moment. A few days before an historic date artist Ninetta Sombart painted an angel who stands above the earth in a gesture of despair, shocked by the deeds of human beings. Sombart had painted many angels in her life, but never an angel in despair. Only when a few days later, on September 11, 2001, the Twin Towers in New York were changed into a ruin and almost 3,000 people lost their lives, did she understand what she had painted. She gave the painting the title: September 11 Angel.

Figure 14.1: September 11 Angel, Ninetta Sombart.

Even God has to watch impotently what people do to each other and to the earth. The anonymous poem 'Waiting for a Miracle', which was mentioned in Chapter 1, ends with a question of the 'powerless' God:

How can I save without your hands?
How can I judge without your voices?
How can I love without your hearts?
From the seventh day I put everything into your hands,
My whole creation and my power.

It is not you, but I who is waiting for a miracle.

God has given the earth to human beings (Ps 115:16) and surrendered part of his omnipotence so that we might become co-creators. In Chapter 1 we learned that the Jewish mystical tradition, the Kabbalah, has a special word for this deed of divine restraint: *tzimtzum*. Most of the time, however, we have a much too primitive picture of the all-powerful God. In the lecture 'Love and Its Significance in the World', Rudolf Steiner formulated this as follows:

> God is pure and total love, not the highest wisdom nor the mightiest power. God retained the love but shared the power and wisdom with Ahriman and Lucifer respectively: power with Ahriman, wisdom with Lucifer, so that human beings might be free and, under the influence of wisdom, take their onward course.[1]

Rudolf Frieling once pictured the impotence of the spiritual world on earth by imagining a young bird that has fallen out of its nest. The little bird is helpless, and so is the mother. The angels cannot lift it up with their hands, and the cat cannot do anything other than eat it. We human beings are the only ones who can lift it up and put it back into its nest.

The human being thus has possibilities that have not been given to any other creature, neither in heaven nor on earth. This brings us to the spiritual dimension of the question: what can I do for the earth and its future?

When we ask ourselves this question, we can feel impotent in the face of the challenges confronting us as individuals. This is sometimes called 'apocalypse fatigue'. In response to this we might wish to close the door to all the hardship in the world. Virtual reality offers us a way to do this: allowing us to retreat into our own make-believe world, into the cocoon of the metaverse, where we can shut out the intrusive and disturbing reality. Another response it to try and find a scapegoat, someone to blame, whether it's the government, industry, the G7, some big foundation or secret brotherhoods. This can quickly lead to us becoming lost in conspiracy theories and disinformation, spreading lies that undermine reality.

If we manage to avoid responding in this way, we are still left with the question of what to do about it. A well-known slogan of recent times is, 'a better environment begins with ourselves'. There are numerous websites that recommend all sorts of measures we can adopt such as turning off the tap while brushing your teeth, recycling, walking and bicycling instead of using the car, eating organic food, and so on. And yet despite all of this advice, the problem still remains.

Getting to the root of the problem requires effort. What is really causing this crisis?

James Gustave Speth, environmental lawyer and advisor on environmental problems to US presidents Jimmy Carter and Bill Clinton, arrived at the following insight:

> I thought that the most important problems of the
> environment were loss of biodiversity, collapse of the
> ecosystem, climate change. I thought that with thirty years of
> science in this field we could deal with these problems. But
> I was wrong. The most important environmental problems
> are egoism, greed, and apathy. To solve this problem we need
> a spiritual and cultural transformation and we, legal and
> scientific experts, do not know how to do that.[2]

Science by itself is not capable of turning the tide of the exploitation of the environment, because the most important environmental problems are egoism, greed and apathy.

Jacques Lusseyran provided the most fundamental answer to this problem in his book *Against the Pollution of the I*, which he wrote just before his death. In it he explained that what we call our I in daily life is most of the time a caricature: it is the ego that wants to live at the expense of others. According to Lusseyran, 'By giving the ego free rein, the I is put to death.'[3] In our current, everyday world we don't have an I-culture, but rather an ego-culture. Our actual I is more and more occupied, or even possessed, by the world that washes over us every day: advertising, news, entertainment, social media, addiction. All of this pushes its way into the hidden Holy of Holies of the human being and the result is that we no longer think and act freely. This is the real cause of the pollution of the earth. The I can only truly express itself when it is able to act out of its own initiative, guided by conscience. But its own activity has been weakened or even paralysed. As Lusseyran puts it: 'Our I is fragile because invariably it diminishes when it is not active.'[4]

The true I is in danger of being obscured by the everyday troubles of earth existence. In the Offertory during the Consecration of the Human Being this warning goes out to human beings: 'that they bury not their eternal being for the sake of their temporal'. Lusseyran's call is therefore a plea to guard our threshold and, whenever something demands our attention, to listen to ourselves rather than to hidden tempters.

With the qualities of our soul life – thinking, feeling and willing – we always create an atmosphere around ourselves. Over time this communicates itself to the people with whom we share our space, consciously or unconsciously. In this way we either create a salutary climate or a climate crisis, in both the literal and figurative sense of the words.

Lusseyran wrote about the visible consequences of the pollution of the I. In *How to Know Higher Worlds*, Rudolf Steiner writes about the invisible consequences, which can be at least equally dramatic. In the chapter on the requirements for esoteric training he gives seven conditions for the path of inner schooling. You might also call them seven methods for inner hygiene. According to the third requirement:

> The pupil must be able to work his way to the realisation that his thoughts and feelings are as important for the world as his actions. He must recognise that it is just as harmful to hate a fellow being as to strike him. The knowledge then comes to me that when I strive to improve myself, I accomplish something not only for myself but also for the world. The world derives as much benefit from my unsullied feelings and thoughts as from my good conduct. As long as I cannot believe in this importance of my inner life for the world I am not fit to be an esoteric pupil. I shall be imbued with the right belief in the significance of my inner self, of my soul, when I work at it as though it were at least as real as anything external. I must come to admit that every feeling has as real an effect as an action of my hand.[5]

With everything we do we first of all have to cultivate our inner life. This is the prerequisite for transforming the outer world. In Chapter 9 we learned that morality is the true seed for the future – not only for our own future but for the future of the earth. By the way I think and feel, speak and act, I create the conditions not just of my future incarnation, but the future of the earth. Everything that lives in us will become our environment. Steiner stated: 'The future resides in the hearts of men and women.'[6]

Psychotherapist and child psychologist Haim Ginott came to a similar conclusion in a completely different way. As a psychologist and pedagogue, he not only studied the relationships between parents and children, but also between teachers and children. He published the results of his study in his book *Between Parent and Child*, in which he wrote:

I have come to the disturbing conclusion that I am the critical element in the class. It is my personal approach that creates the climate. It is my daily mood that causes the weather.[7]

It is interesting that he uses the word 'climate' here as well as 'weather' to describe the spiritual environment in a class. He goes on to say:

I possess tremendous power to make life in the class miserable or joyful. I can be an instrument of torture or of inspiration. I can humiliate or alleviate, injure or heal. In all situations it is my response that decides whether a crisis will escalate or de-escalate, whether a person is strengthened or weakened in his humanity.[8]

It sounds simple enough: create your own world. But how do you do that in an environment that robs you of your freedom? Are you still able to strengthen your humanity in an inhuman world?

Etty Hillesum was one of those people who, in the hell of a death camp in the Second World War, fought ceaselessly against the pollution of the I. In her diary she shows how, with her thoughts and feelings, she created an atmosphere of attention and empathy, in which everyone around her was included:

At night, when I was lying there on my plank bed in the midst of women and girls who were softly snoring, dreaming aloud, or silently crying and tossing and turning, and who during the day often said: 'We don't want to think, we don't want to feel, otherwise we go mad,' – then I sometimes felt endless compassion and was lying awake letting the events, the much too many impressions of a much too long day pass before me, and thought: Allow me to be the thinking heart of this barrack. I would like to be the thinking heart of a whole concentration camp.[9]

When a life is not only disturbed, like in Etty Hillesum's case, but also wiped out, it is important to take the quintessence of your existence with you across the threshold, and to leave your most precious accomplishment behind for the living. One of the leaders of The White Rose resistance movement in the Second World War gave an impressive description of this in a dream picture she had on the night before she was condemned to death. The morning she was to be executed Sophie Scholl told her cell mate a dream:

On a sunny day I was carrying a child in a white dress to its baptism. I was walking up a steep mountain toward a church. I had the child firmly in my arms. Suddenly, unexpectedly, a crevice opened in the mountain. I just had time to drop the child on the other side before I fell into the abyss.[10]

It is the task of every human being not to let this child fall into the abyss, but to put it in a safe place before we cross the threshold. Sophie Scholl herself said about this dream: 'The child is our idea; in spite of the obstacles it will be fulfilled. We could be its precursors, but we have to die first for it.'

We are led even further through the dying process by the experiences of Dannion Brinkley, a Vietnam veteran who lost himself in the trauma of war, thoughtlessly and mechanically killing and plundering.[11] Back in America he had a near-death experience that placed all the events of his life in a different light. Down to the smallest details he could see them before him again in the panorama of his life. But now he was not only shown his own deeds, but also their far-reaching consequences. He saw himself again, standing at the edge of a rice field and shooting into a village, massacring part of the population. Whether he wanted to or not, he slipped into the skin of his victims and felt their pain, their consternation – and the grief of the survivors. Every deed had a chain of consequences, which only now made him realise what he did.

After the war, Brinkley worked as a soldier in Africa. He had to deliver weapons at an airport. In the retrospective view of his life, he saw not only the physical act, but also its consequences in the countless lives that were destroyed in wartime violence. Among the overwhelming experiences of his guilt, however, one event appeared – almost too insignificant to pay attention to – that formed a spot of light in the review. Back in the United States one afternoon he was walking through New York. A few Vietnamese beggars were rummaging through trash looking for food. In a fit of compassion, he invited them to a restaurant and gave them a meal, and experienced the gratefulness the beggars felt for this meal. It was this experience that made him realise what is important in life on earth: 'What you did for the least of My brethren…'

With these impressions he came back into life from his near-death experience and was able to build a new existence.

The experiences of Etty Hillesum, Sophie Scholl and Dannion Brinkley demonstrate that it is possible to do something even in seemingly impossible circumstances. I cannot decide for someone else what he or she must do. Perhaps nothing 'must' be done; perhaps every event in our lives gives us possibilities that we use or fail to use. But one thing we can do is to develop and practise methods in our life that enable us to be fully present to those moments when we *can* do something.

In Chapter 12, I mentioned that Rudolf Steiner speaks about sensitising our conscience. The voice of conscience is a silent counsellor that suggests to us what we can do in a particular situation. Whether we then do it and how we do it – that is our choice. Our moral intuition gives us no commands or prohibitions but asks us to act in the situation. In many cases this also means acting spontaneously in ways we might not otherwise do, such as when Dannion Brinkley acted on an impulse of generosity. In some cases this may save lives and totally change a desperate situation.

So far, the attempt to answer the question 'What can I do?' can seem to lead to a very lonely experience. We are likely to feel thrown back on ourselves when we try to answer it. It is clear that as individuals we are not capable of doing all that needs to be done to turn the tide. In *The Fairy Tale of the Green Snake and the Beautiful Lily* by Goethe, the old man with the lamp says to the lily: 'One sole person does not help, but whoever unites himself with many at the right time.' The answer, in other words, lies in the principle of community.

In Africa this concept of community is expressed in the Bantu languages using the term *Ubuntu*. Loosely translated it means 'I am because we are'. Just as there is no 'we' without 'I', so there is no 'I' without 'we'. Nelson Mandela, who frequently used the concept of *Ubuntu*, often gave an example how it works in practice. When an unknown traveller walks into an African village, half the population comes out. When the visitor is hungry, tired, or thirsty, the inhabitants will offer them food, drink and shelter.

The idea of community is also expressed in the imagery of the Apocalypse with the imagination of the New Jerusalem. Just as a city on earth without people becomes an empty shell, the New Jerusalem is inconceivable without the 'great assembly which no one could count, from all peoples and tribes and races and languages' (Rev. 7:9), which, through earthly trials, have laid the foundations prepared of a future creation. Any time a complete community is indicated in the New Testament, the symbolism of twelve, or a multiple of it, is used: the twelve disciples, the 144,000, the twelve gates of the New Jerusalem. Only when the individual unites themselves with others in a culture of unselfishness at the right moment, then does the future perspective of the New Jerusalem come into view.

An indication of such a future form of community was once given in a conversation between Rudolf Steiner and Ernst Lehrs. Ernst Lehrs reported on this as follows: 'Rudolf Steiner said in a personal conversation, "When a number of conscious people find each other in a well-disposed exchange they can accomplish together what for a single person only becomes possible by initiation."'[12]

I understand this rather cryptic remark to mean that, while in our time it is only possible for single individuals to experience initiation, nevertheless, when people work consciously together in a community, they can accomplish what otherwise could only be brought about by an initiate. The principle of this form of initiation is unselfish cooperation. Rudolf Steiner once said something similar in a lecture. With just a single sentence he indicated that even in the greatest chaos a creation out of nothing is possible:

> If a sad age dawned across the globe when millions and millions of people passed their days devoid of spirituality ... the earth would however still shine out in solar, spiritual radiance if only a dozen people still possessed lucid, moral and spiritual enthusiasm.[13]

These words express the perspective of the hierarchies. Wherever on earth people think and act morally, even in a world of moral decline, the angels recognise the seeds of the future New Jerusalem. Again, the decisive aspect is that even if there is only a little group of people who create this unselfish community, the earth can still be spiritualised and reach its destination. Here, too, the number twelve points to a complete, perfect community.

When people live and work together in a community it then becomes possible for a higher being to express itself through the members of that community. According to Steiner, people who think and feel harmoniously together are more than just the sum of their number:

> People living and striving together signifies something very similar to the living into each other of the cells of the human body. A new, higher being stands in the midst of the five – or even just two or three, as Christ says in Matthew's Gospel: 'For where two or three gather in my name, there am I with them'

(Matt. 18:29). It is not the one and the other and the third, but something entirely new that comes into being through community. But it comes into being only if the individual lives in the other, when the individual derives their forces not only from themselves but also from the other. And that can only happen if they live selflessly with each other. Thus, human communities are mysterious places into which higher spiritual beings descend, in order to work through individual human beings, just as the soul works through the members of the body.

In our materialistic age people will not easily believe this, but in the spiritual-scientific world view it is not just a picture but in the highest degree real. Therefore, the spiritual scientist does not just speak of abstract things when he speaks of the folk spirit or folk soul, or of the family spirit or the spirit of a community. One cannot see this spirit that works in a community, but it is there, and it is there through the brotherly love of the personalities working in this community. Just as the body has a soul, a guild, a brotherhood also has a soul, and I repeat, this is not just a picture, but has to be understood as actual truth.[14]

We can also extend this definition of community to include our deceased loved ones. Just as we were connected with them during life, after their death they are also engaged in our weal and woe and can give us counsel with their insights. We must therefore ask ourselves: are we open and sensitive to their inspirations, and are we able to act on them?

Apart from the 'karmic group' to which we belong, there are also the Masters of Wisdom and Harmony of Feelings, the great initiates who work ceaselessly on earth and in the spiritual world on behalf of humanity. When Friedrich Rittelmeyer asked Rudolf Steiner, 'Where are the initiates now?' Steiner replied: 'If you were to meet these Initiates today you might not find in them anything that you are seeking.'[15]

Something similar is described in the Jewish tradition of the Lamed-Waf, the just. The Talmud relates that there are 36 just, or righteous ones always living on the earth at any one time. When one of them dies, a new Lamed-Waf is born to replace them. According to tradition, they are so just that they do not know of themselves that they are just. But if one of them was missing, the world would perish. For their sake God preserves the world, even if the rest of humanity sinks into barbarism. According to Steiner:

> Those who work together in mutual help are magicians
> because they pull in higher beings ... If we give ourselves up
> to mutual help, through this giving up to the community a
> powerful strengthening of our being takes place. If we then
> speak or act as a member of such a community there speaks
> or acts in us not the singular soul only but the spirit of the
> community. This is the secret of progress for the future of
> humanity: to work out of communities.[16]

The foregoing observations show that with moral deeds we are in the good company of our conscience ('the Christ-voice of our conscience,' says Rudolf Steiner), of our dear deceased, and finally, together with all of humanity, of the great initiates. An army of helpers stands ready on the other side of the threshold to assist us on our lonely path. Lonely but not alone. Above them there are even larger armies to stand by us. This way up into the spiritual world culminates in the Godhead who encompasses everything. Ultimately, notwithstanding divine impotence, everything is in his hands.

The service of the Consecration of the Human Being has a unique formulation for this, which expresses God's hidden omnipotence: He 'fulfils the revelation, the ordering of space, the course of time.' In the chaos of space and time a hidden order is working. In all that reveals itself in our life, in all the events that take place in space and time, He is present. The Godhead 'is in all that we are'.[17] An aspect of this all-encompassing presence is expressed in one of the psalms in the verse, 'My times are in your hands' (Ps. 31:15). Every moment of my life is in the hands of the Godhead.

Rudolf Frieling once turned this sentence around and came to the original thought: not only is my time in your hands, but your time is also in my hands.[18] What can I do with the time I have been given in my life? Every moment of my life is a gift that the divine world has given me. Can I use it in such a way that it becomes a service to the divine world? When you become conscious of this, every moment becomes precious. It is in this sense of the word that all the great saints, initiates and moral giants have always worked. As Mahatma Gandhi wrote: 'You may not waste a grain of rice or a scrap of paper, and similarly a minute of your time.'[19]

Afterword

Looking back over what I have written I am coming to a paradoxical conclusion: I am viewing the future with growing concern and with growing confidence. It is probably not necessary to write once again where my concern comes from. Everywhere we hear today that things are going totally wrong.

But where do I get my confidence from? While everywhere on earth the weeds are thriving, there are at the same time also hopeful germs growing for the future. Together with signs of uncontrolled growth, decline and destruction, when you look beyond the outer reality you can recognise seeds for the future that grow out of new initiatives and confidence in the always present help of the spiritual world.

In a delicate way a Hassidic legend illustrates what is needed to save us and our world for the future:

In a dream I walked into a shop and asked: 'What are you selling here?'

The angel who served me said: 'Whatever you may want.'

'If that is true then I want peace on earth, an end to repression and hunger, homes for all refugees, and...'

'Wait,' said the angel. 'You misunderstand me. We sell no fruits here. We sell only seeds.'

Appendix

Every year, the Dutch newspaper *Trouw* publishes *The Sustainable One Hundred*, their list of one hundred organisations and individuals who have, in one way or another, established a sustainable initiative. These often include individual citizens who work together to come up with solutions for environmental problems. For example, in 2021, members of one of the largest public employee pension funds got together to demand that the fund become 'fossil-free'. This fund covers teachers, government employees and agents who no longer wanted their pensions invested in fossil fuels. They threatened the fund with legal action and since 2022 it no longer invests in petroleum and coal.

But this excellent story has a big footnote. For what is happening elsewhere? What will the rest of the financial world do? There are investors who, in reaction to this initiative, invested large amounts in oil and coal production, so that the exploitation of the earth can continue unimpeded. We must not have any illusions about the usefulness of individual initiatives. Every time we see that other banks and pension funds pick up where others left off. James Otto, one of the leaders of Friends of the Earth, wrote recently:

> Dutch banks and insurance companies continue to finance
> industrial plantations in my country, Liberia, on a large scale.
> This is far from honest and sustainable banking. These palm
> oil plantations gobble up the last remaining large tracts of the
> rain forest of Upper Guinea. Millions of my compatriots have
> lost their economic security because they live off the forest

and the land. Therefore, I ask the Dutch government to hold those entities and lenders responsible for the environmental damage and human rights violations in Liberia and elsewhere … When someone gets a job on those plantations they have to work with dangerous pesticides and herbicides, the working conditions are terrible, and the pay is too little to live on. One group of sixteen villagers was thrown into prison for more than a year when they protested against the seizure of their land. Peasants who demand the return of their land are criminalised. Drinking water is polluted and communities that are dependent on the forests lose their source of income. We have written to the banks but receive no answers. They don't take any action, not even after obvious proof of human rights violations and deforestation.

With this report the writer calls on the Dutch government to take action. So far, he has been met with silence. It is just business as usual.[1]

Another initiative on the list of one hundred sustainable actions is called 'Stop Ecocide Nederland', which forms part of the international organisation Rights of Nature. This is a group of lawyers who are trying to get nature treated as an actual person. Violations against the environment have sometimes received recognition in the International Court of Justice, and in a few countries, such as Ecuador, these rights have already been accorded. Nature is treated legally as a person, hence the name Rights of Nature.

A third sustainable initiative is 'Advertising Fossil-Free', a group that breaks up 'all the green castles in the sky' of companies that incorrectly announce that they are doing something for the environment. For example, not so long ago the oil giant Shell claimed that customers could offset their carbon emissions by paying four cents more a gallon, effectively making their cars climate neutral. However, in a subsequent court case Shell had to distance itself from this misleading advertising and was ordered to cut emissions.[2]

Important work is also being done by Paul Hawken. Since the 1960s he has worked as an environmental activist and as 'champion for ethical enterprise' in the areas of organic food, green energy, and even green chemistry. Along with two hundred researchers and advisors, Hawken has spent years looking for the most effective solutions to the climate problem. In his book *Drawdown* he describes in order of effectiveness a hundred different possibilities to stop the climate crisis and bring about a reversal in global warming. He not only looks at the impact each solution would have, but also at the investments needed to carry it out and its financial return. Hawken doesn't want to talk about the problems, but about solutions.

According to Project Drawdown, the measure that yields the greatest result is the reduction of cooling liquids in refrigerators and air conditioners.[3] When it was discovered in the 1980s that these chemicals (CFCs and HCFCs) damage the ozone layer, their production was largely stopped, but 90% of these chemical emissions take place when these appliances are processed after they have been junked. Since then, technologies have been developed to neutralise cooling liquids and reduce them to chemicals that have no effects on the climate or ozone layer. Unfortunately, the technologies created to produce cooling liquids have created a new problem because they consist of very strong greenhouse gasses that are ten times more polluting than CO_2.

The second most effective solution suggested by Project Drawdown is wind energy. We often hear about the high level of subsidies needed to create wind energy on a large scale without realising how these compare to the subsidies received by the fossil-fuel industry. The International Monetary Fund has calculated that worldwide the wind energy industry has received subsidies of $12.3 billion (£9.7 billion) since the year 2000. By contrast, the fossil-fuel industry received $5.3 trillion (£4.1 trillion) in direct and indirect subsidies in 2015 alone!

The third solution that makes a big difference is the reduction of food waste. In rich countries especially, food is wasted on a large scale. One third of food that is produced does not reach the consumer, and such waste contributes 8% of the total CO_2 emissions.

The report not only describes and calculates the results for the environment of well-known measures such as solar energy, climate-neutral construction and reforestation. It also analyses less conventional ideas such as seaweed nurseries, green roofs that insulate, infrastructure for bicycles and so on.[4]

One of the most noteworthy conclusions of the Project Drawdown is to let girls go to school. What does that have to do with climate change? When girls, in lieu of doing child labour, get the opportunity to go to school, learn a trade, and start a family, experience shows that because of birth control and family planning, family sizes tend to be smaller.

All these ideas, however, depend entirely on what may be called the engine of the climate crisis, which is the dogma of unlimited growth. This dogma is a seven-headed dragon: when you cut off one head, two new ones grow elsewhere. When we see successful climate initiatives in one area, somewhere else things are getting significantly worse. We encounter this kind of mentality in the Apocalypse of St John where we come across the recurring phrase, '...they refused to repent of what they had done' (Rev. 16:11). This does not mean that all the efforts on the part of those who want to save our earth are in vain, on the contrary. But there is a part of our humanity that does not want to learn. That is the sobering message of the Apocalypse.

The dogma of unlimited growth, brings me to interesting initiatives that have a renewing effect on the economy. These initiatives are often summarised under the term 'doughnut economics', or 'regenerative economics'. In her book *Doughnut Economics*, economist Kate Raworth describes a pair of concentric rings that make up the regenerative economy. The inner ring she calls the 'social foundation', which is concerned with human well-being and the provision of food, education and shelter. Below this foundation 'lie critical human deprivations such as hunger and illiteracy'. The outer ring is the 'ecological ceiling'. It represents the boundary to economic growth beyond which we exceed our ecological footprint and cause harm to the environment. Between these two is the area of the actual economy, where human beings can thrive without causing unsustainable damage either to society or to the planet.[5]

Remarkably, this international initiative was introduced for the first time in Amsterdam. Since April 2020 the City Council has worked with a model of the regenerative economy with the goal that in due time all inhabitants of the city will stay within the confines of the social foundation (a home for everyone, education, schooling and so on), and where at the same time the local economy stays within the limits of the ecological ceiling. Amsterdam is the cradle of the capitalistic economy. The Amsterdam stock exchange is the oldest in the world. In 1602 shares in the Dutch East India Company were sold for the first time in history. That was the beginning of what we now know as the Amsterdam Stock Exchange. In New Amsterdam – now New York – this form of economy became huge. Instead of economic growth as the highest goal of capitalism, the goal of the regenerative economy is to include both human beings and the environment in its considerations.

Notes

Foreword
1. Truman, *Memoirs of Harry S. Truman, Vol.1*, p 11.
2. Steiner, *At the Gates of Spiritual Science*, Answers to Questions, September 2, 1906, p. 145.

1. Signs of the Times
1. Steiner, 'The Soul's Awakening', Scene 11, in *Four Mystery Dramas*, p. 127.
2. Scharmer, *Theory U: Leading from the Future as It Emerges*.
3. The term 'post-truth' was chosen as The Oxford Dictionary's word of the year for 2016.
4. Steiner, *Sprüche, Dichtungen, Mantren, Ergänzungsband: Nachträge, Handschriften* [Proverbs, Poems, Mantras: Supplementary Volume – Addendums, Manuscripts].

2. What Do Mythologies Say About the Future?
1. Plato, *Phaedrus*.
2. Müller, *Lectures on the Science of Language*.
3. Steiner, *The Presence of the Dead on the Spiritual Path*, lecture of April 17, 1914, p. 93.
4. Steiner, *Spiritual Science as a Foundation for Social Forms*, lecture of September 11, 1920, pp. 264f.
5. *Prana* means 'breath of life' or 'life force'.
6. Plato was the first to report the downfall of Atlantis (literally: 'Island of Atlas') in his dialogues *Timaeus* and *Critias*. The name of Atlantis occurs earlier in the works of philosopher Anaximander (circa 610–546 BC) and historian Herodotus (circa 485–25 BC).

3. Old Forms of Predicting the Future: Prophets, Sibyls and Shamans

1. A Greek theologian in the Byzantine Empire in the sixth century AD who produced a series of writings of a mystical nature. They were originally attributed to Dionysius the Areopagite, the Athenian convert of St Paul mentioned in Acts 17:34, but were later declared to be pseudonymous works. He became known as pseudo-Dionysius.

2. Steiner, *Vorträge und Kurse über christlich-religiöses Wirken* [Lectures and Courses on Christian Religious Work], lecture of September 11, 1922.

3. Heraclitus, *Fragments*, Fragment 92.

4. Lagerlöf, *Christ Legends*, pp. 16f.

5. See Cassius Dio, *The Roman History: The Reign of Augustus*.

6. Steiner, *Christ and the Spiritual World*, lecture of December 29, 1913, pp. 48f.

7. Steiner, *Four Mystery Dramas*. See also lecture of September 19, 1915, in *The Value of Thinking* about Theodora's clairvoyance.

8. Jung, *Memories, Dreams, Reflections*, p. 313.

4. The Little Apocalypse

1. Madrigal, Marc, 'The Gospel of the King: What did the "Lordship" of Jesus mean for the first century Christians?', *Evangelical Focus*, April 4, 2019, www.evangelicalfocus.com/ archaeological-perspectives/4343/the-gospel-of-the-king.

2. So called by Gregorius, Bishop of Tours in the sixth century.

3. Ritchie, *Return from Tomorrow*.

5. The Apocalypse of St John

1. Steiner, *Die Theosophie an Hand des Johannes Evangeliums* [Theosophy and the Gospel of John], lecture of November 6, 1906.

2. Steiner, *Christianity as Mystical Fact*, p. 94.

3. Steiner, *The Apocalypse of St John*, lecture of June 20, 1908, p. 73.

4. Lusseyran, *Against the Pollution of the I*, p. 83.

5. Steiner, *Christianity as Mystical Fact*, pp. 93f.

6. Steiner, *The Inner Experiences of Evolution*, lecture of November 14, 1911, pp. 40f.
7. Steiner, *Mantric Sayings*, p. ix. See also *Verses and Meditations*, p. 119.
8. Lecture of September 18, 1922, contained in GA344.
9. Pablo Picasso in an open letter published in 1926.
10. Steiner, *Approaching the Mystery of Golgotha*, lecture of June 1, 1914.
11. Steiner, *From Limestone to Lucifer*, Q&A of May 7, 1923, p. 203.
12. Kiessig, *Dichter erzählen ihre Träume* [Poets Tell Their Dreams].
13. See Anna Samweber, *Memories of Rudolf Steiner and Marie Steiner-von Sivers*.
14. Steiner, *Truth-Wrought-Words*, p. 48.

6. Freedom and Inevitability
1. Steiner, *The Mystery of the Trinity*, lecture of August 22, 1922, p. 101.
2. See Isaiah Berlin, *Liberty*.
3. Steiner, 'Michael's Task in the Sphere of Ahriman', in *Anthroposophical Leading Thoughts*, pp. 71–74.
4. Steiner, *Problems of Society*, lectures of October 27 and November 4, 1919.

7. The Counterstream of Time
1. See Steiner, *The Spiritual Guidance of the Individual and Humanity*, lecture two.
2. Eduard Schuré recorded this conversation in the so-called Barr Document, named after the village at the foot of the Vosges mountains where he met Rudolf Steiner in 1907.
3. See Annie Gerding-Le Comte, *Kabouters, gnomen, fantomen. Ontmoetingen met natuurwezens* [Trolls, Gnomes, Phantoms. Encounters with Nature Beings], Lemniscaat, 1979.
4. See Otto Scharmer, *Theory U*, also *Leading from the Future* and *Presence*.

8. Providence: The Hidden Presence of Christ

   1. Goulson, Dave, 'The insect apocalypse: "Our world will grind to a halt without them"', *The Guardian*, July 25, 2021, www.theguardian.com/environment/2021/jul/25/the-insect-apocalypse-our-world-will-grind-to-a-halt-without-them.

   2. Silesius, Angelus, *Der cherubinische Wandersmann* [The Cherubinic Wanderer].

   3. www.operafolio.com.

   4. Steiner, *The Spiritual Guidance of the Individual and Humanity*, p. 5.

   5. Ibid., p. 9

   6. Ibid., p. 14.

   7. From the diary of Gabrielle Bossis, September 16, 1948.

   8. Emmichoven, *The Reality in Which We Live*.

9. 'Behold I Make All Things New': Morality as a Creative Principle

   1. www.decorrespondent.nl.

   2. Cowen, Tyler, 'Policing Nature', in *Environmental Ethics* 25, 2003.

   3. Geoghegan, Tom, 'Toby Ord: Why I'm giving £1m to charity', December 13, 2010, www.bbc.com/news/magazine-11950843.

   4. Steiner, *Study of Man*, lecture of August 23, 1919, p. 43.

   5. See Steiner, *Occult Science*, Chapter 6: The Present and Future of Cosmic Evolution.

   6. Steiner, *Cosmosophy*, lecture of September 23, 1921, p. 9.

   7. Ibid.

   8. Ibid., pp 19f.

   9. See Steiner, *At the Gates of Spiritual Science*, lecture of September 4, 1906.

  10. See Steiner, *The Interior of the Earth* for a more detailed description of these layers.

  11. Steiner, *At the Gates of Spiritual Science*, lecture of September 4, 1906

10. Our Self-created Destiny
    1. Steiner, *An Esoteric Cosmology*, lecture of June 14, 1906, p. 105.
    2. Steiner, *Reading the Pictures of the Apocalypse*, lecture of June 14, 1906, p. 142
    3. Ibid., p. 142f.
    4. Ibid., p. 143.
    5. Boehme, *The Mysterium Magnum*, see Chapter 10: Of the Creation of Heaven and the Outward World.
    6. Rittelmeyer, *Rudolf Steiner Enters My Life*, p. 52f.
    7. Steiner, 'The Soul's Awakening', Scene Eleven, in *Four Mystery Dramas*.
    8. See steinerdatenbank.de.
    9. Steiner, *Vorträge und Kurse über christlich-religiöses Wirken* [Lectures and Courses on Christian Religious Work], lecture of September 30, 1921.
    10. Steiner, *Original Impulses for the Science of the Spirit*, lecture of October 8, 1906, p 97.
    11. Steiner, *The Essentials of Education*, lecture of April 11, 1924, p. 82.
    12. Steiner, *Understanding Society*, lecture of November 1, 1919, p. 152.
    13. Steiner, *Foundations of Esotericism*, lecture of October 17, 1905, p. 145.
    14. 'Black Magic', *Wikipedia*, November, 20 2023, https://en.wikipedia.org/wiki/Black_magic.
    15. 'Schwarze und weisse Magie' [Black and White Magic], *Flensburger Hefte*, Special Issue No.12, 1993.

11. Manichaeism and the Origins of Evil
    1. Steiner, *The Temple Legend*, lecture of November 11, 1904, p. 59.

12. Manichaeism and the Redemption of Evil
    1. Haccohen, *Touching Heaven, Touching Earth*.
    2. Rudolf Steiner notebook 1906, archive no. B105.
    3. Gandhi, *The Collected Works of Mahatma Gandhi, Vol 21*, p. 252.
    4. Bakels, *Nacht und Nebel*.

5. Quoted in Lievegoed, Bernard, *The Eye of the Needle*, Hawthorn Press, UK 1993.

6. Steiner, *The Temple Legend*, lecture of November 11, 1904, p. 66.

7. For example, see lecture of February 3, 1912, in *Three Paths to Christ*.

8. 'Terminal Lucidity', *Wikipedia*, March, 20, 2024, https://en.wikipedia.org/wiki/Terminal_lucidity.

9. Morgenstern, Christian *Wir fanden einen Pfad* [We Have Found a Path].

13. Current Trends and Developments

1. Oltmans, Willem, *Grenzen aan de groei , deel 1. 75 gesprekken over de Club van Rome* [Limits to Growth, Part 1: 75 Conversations About the Club of Rome], A.W. Bruna & Zoon, Holland 1973, p. 414.

2. 'Prosperity Theology', *Wikipedia*, April 3, 2024, available at: https://en.wikipedia.org/wiki/Prosperity_theology.

3. 'Planetary Boundaries', Stockholm Resilience Centre, www.stockholmresilience.org/research/planetary-boundaries.html.

4. Nikiforuk, Andrew, 'Buzz Holling's Resilient Universe', *Resilience*, December 4, 2019, www.resilience.org/stories/2019-12-04/buzz-hollings-resilient-universe.

5. Goethe, *Naturwissenschaftlichte Schriften. Die Natur, Fragment* [Natural Scientific Writings: A Fragment].

6. See Nina Schick, *Deep Fakes and the Infocalypse* and Nicanor Perlas, *Humanity's Last Stand*.

7. 'The Metaverse and How We'll Build It Together – Connect 2021', www.youtube.com/watch?v=Uvufun6xer8.

8. Kreye, Andrian, 'Was kommt nach dem Handy' [What Comes After the Cellphone?], *Süddeutsche Zeitung*, October 1, 2021, available at: www.sueddeutsche.de/projekte/artikel/digital/was-kommt-nach-dem-handy-e209713/?reduced=true.

9. Gatehouse, G., *The Coming Storm*, BBC Radio 4, www.bbc.co.uk/programmes/m001324r/episodes/downloads.

10. Harari, *Homo Deus: A Brief History of Tomorrow*.

11. Ruth Scherpenhuijsen Rom, *Hebräische Notizen* in: *Die Christengemeinschaft,* September 1994, Stuttgart.
12. Harari, *Homo Deus.*
13. Agarwal, Sujata, 'Nanobots: Futuristic MedTech That Can Change Healthcare Today', *Epam*, 3 November 2021, www.epam.com/insights/blogs/nanobots-futuristic-medtech-that-can-change-healthcare-today.
14. See *Jonas*, June 12, 1981.

14. What Can I Do?

1. Steiner, *Three Paths to Christ*, lecture of December 17, 1912, p. 176f.
2. *Shared Planet: Religion and Nature*, BBC Radio 4, October 1, 2013.
3. Lusseyran, *Against the Pollution of the I.*
4. Ibid.
5. Steiner, *Knowledge of the Higher Worlds*, p. 82.
6. Steiner, *Reading the Pictures of the Apocalypse*, lecture of June 14, 1906, p. 142.
7. Ginott, *Between Parent and Child.*
8. Ibid.
9. Hillesum, *An Interrupted Life.*
10. Selg, *Der geistige Weg von Hans und Sophie Scholl* [The Spiritual Path of Hand and Sophie Scholl], p. 122.
11. See Dannion Brinkley, *Saved by the Light.*
12. *Mitteilungen aus der anthroposophischen Arbeit in Deutschland* [Messages from Anthroposophical Work in Germany], no. 37, 1956.
13. Steiner, *Universal Spirituality and Human Physicality*, lecture of December 18, 1920, p. 148.
14. Steiner, *Die Welträtsel und die Anthroposophie* [The Riddles of the World and Anthroposophy], lecture of November 23, 1905.
15. Rittelmeyer, *Rudolf Steiner Enters My Life*, p. 96.
16. Steiner, *Die Welträtsel und die Anthroposophie* [The Riddles of the World and Anthropsophy], lecture of November 23, 1905.

17. The Christian Community, Service of the Consecration of the Human Being, Trinitarian Epistle.
18. Frieling, *The Complete Old Testament Studies*, p. 303.
19. Gandhi, *The Collected Works of Mahatma Gandhi, Vol 26*, p. 272.

Appendix

1. Otto, James D, 'With Dutch Money the Forest Disappears', *Trouw*, October 26, 2021.
2. 'Shell: Netherlands court orders oil giant to cut emissions', *BBC*, 26 May 2021, available at: https://www.bbc.co.uk/news/world-europe-57257982.
3. Anyone who wants to follow the principal findings of Hawken's research in detail should go to: https://greenamerica.org/climate-change-100-reasons-hope/top-10-solutions-reverse-climate-change.
4. In Holland, which has a good infrastructure for bicycles, 28% of local trips are made by bicycle. In America the figure is 1% because there are hardly any bicycle lanes.
5. Haworth, *Doughnut Economics*, p. 10f.

Bibliography

Bakels, Floris, *Nacht Und Nebel* [Night and Fog], Lutterworth Press, UK 2000.

Berlin, Isaiah, *Liberty*, (ed. Henry Hardy), Oxford University Press, UK 2002.

Bock, Emil, *Caesars and Apostles*, Floris Books, UK 2018.

Brinkley, Dannion, *Saved by the Light: The True Story of a Man Who Died Twice and the Profound Revelations He Received*, HarperOne, USA 2008.

Campbell, Joseph, *The Hero's Journey*, New World Library, USA 2014.

—, *The Hero with a Thousand Faces*, New World Library, USA 2012.

Dio, Cassius, *The Roman History: The Reign of Augustus*, Scott-Kilvert, Ian (trans), Penguin Classics, UK 1987.

Emmichoven, F.W. Zeylmans van, *The Reality in Which We Live*, New Knowledge Books, USA 1964.

The Epic of Gilgamesh, (trans. Andrew George), Penguin Classics, UK 1999.

Flowers, Betty Sue, Jaworski, Joseph, Senge, Peter, and Scharmer, Otto C., *Presence: Exploring Profound Change in People, Organizations and Society*, Nicholas Brealey Publishing, UK 2005.

Frankl, Viktor, *Man's Search for Meaning: The Classic Tribute to Hope from the Holocaust*, Beacon Press, USA 2006.

Frieling, Rudolf, *Christianity and Reincarnation*, Floris Books, UK 1977.

—, *The Complete Old Testament Studies*, Floris Books, UK 2022.

Ginott, Haim, *Between Parent and Child*, Random House, UK 1965.

Haccohen, Shmuel Avidor, *Touching Heaven, Touching Earth: Hasidic Humour and Wit*, Sadan Publishing House, USA 1976.

Harari, Yuval Noah, *Homo Deus: A Brief History of Tomorrow*, Vintage, UK 2017.

Hawken, Paul, *Drawdown. The Most Comprehensive Plan Ever Proposed to Reverse Global Warming*, Penguin, UK 2018.

Hillesum, Etty, *An Interrupted Life: The Diaries and Letters of Etty Hillesum 1941–43*, Picador, UK 1996.

Jung, C.G., *Memories, Dreams, Reflections*, Fontana Press, UK 1995.

Kiessig, Martin, *Dichter erzählen ihre Träume: Selbstzeugnisse deutscher Dichter aus zwei Jahrhunderten* [Poets Tell Their Dreams: Testimonies of German Poets from Two Centuries], Urrachaus, Germany 1976.

Lagerlöf, Selma, *Christ Legends*, Floris Books, UK 2013.

Lusseyran, Jacques, *Against the Pollution of the I: On the Gifts of Blindness, the Power of Poetry, and the Urgency of Awareness*, New World Library, USA 2016.

Morgenstern, Christian, *Wir fanden einen Pfad* [We Have Found a Path], (trans. Bruce R.H.), Mercury Press, USA 2013.

Perlas, Nicanor, *Humanity's Last Stand: The Challenge of Artificial Intelligence – A Spiritual-Scientific Response*, Temple Lodge, UK 2018.

Plato, *Phaedrus*, Penguin Classics, UK 2005.

The Poetic Edda, (trans. H. A. Bellows), Dover Publications, USA 2004.

Raworth, Kate, *Doughnut Economics: Seven Ways to Think Like a 21st-Century Economist*, Penguin, UK 2022.

Ritchie, George, *Return from Tomorrow*, Chosen Books, USA 2007.

Rittelmeyer, Friedrich, *Rudolf Steiner Enters My Life*, Floris Books, UK 2022.

Saint-Exupéry, Antoine de, *The Little Prince*, Wordsworth Editions, UK 1995.

Samweber, Anna, *Memories of Rudolf Steiner and Marie Steiner-von Sivers*, Rudolf Steiner Press, UK 2015.

Scharmer, Otto, *Leading from the Future: From Ego-System to Eco-System Economies*, Berrett-Koehler Publishers, USA 2013.

—, *Theory U: Leading from the Future as it Emerges*, Berrett-Koehler Publishers, USA 2016.

Schick, Nina, *Deep Fakes and the Infocalypse: What You Urgently Need to Know*, Monoray, UK 2020.

Selg, Peter, *Der geistige Weg von Hans und Sophie Scholl* [The Spiritual Path of Hand and Sophie Scholl], Verlag am Goetheanum, Switzerland 2006,

Singer, Peter, *The Most Good You Can Do: How Effective Altruism Is Changing Ideas about Living Ethically*, Yale University Press, USA 2015.

Steiner, Rudolf, *Anthroposophical Leading Thoughts* (CW26), Rudolf Steiner Press, UK 1973.

—, *The Apocalypse of St John* (CW104), Rudolf Steiner Press, UK 1993.

—, *Approaching the Mystery of Golgotha* (CW152), SteinerBooks, USA 2006.

—, *Christ and the Spiritual World: The Quest for the Holy Grail* (CW149), Rudolf Steiner Press, UK 2008.

—, *Christianity as Mystical Fact And the Mysteries of Antiquity* (CW8), SteinerBooks, USA 2006.

—, *Cosmosophy: Vol. 1* (CW207), Anthroposophic Press, USA 1985.

—, *Die Theosophie an Hand des Johannes Evangeliums* [Theosophy of the Gospel of St John] (GA94), Rudolf Steiner Verlag, Switzerland 2001.

—, *Die Welträtsel und die Anthroposophie* [The Riddles of the World and Anthroposophy] (GA54), Rudolf Steiner Verlag, Switzerland 1983.

—, *An Esoteric Cosmology: Evolution, Christ and Modern Spirituality* (CW94), SteinerBooks, USA 2008.

—, *The Essentials of Education* (CW308), Anthroposophic Press, USA 1997.

—, *Foundation of Esotericism* (CW93a), Rudolf Steiner Press, UK 1983.

—, *Four Mystery Dramas* (CW14), SteinerBooks, USA 2007.

—, *From Limestone to Lucifer... Answers to Questions* (CW349), Rudolf Steiner Press, UK 1999.

—, *How to Know Higher Worlds* (CW10), Anthroposophic Press, USA 1994.

—, *The Inner Experiences of Evolution* (CW132), SteinerBooks, USA 2010.

—, *The Interior of the Earth: An Esoteric Study of the Subterranean Spheres*, Rudolf Steiner Press, UK 2006.

—, *Mantric Sayings Meditations: 1903–1925* (CW268), SteinerBooks, USA 2015.

—, *The Mystery of the Trinity and the Mission of the Spirit* (CW214), SteinerBooks, USA 2016.

—, *Occult Science: An Outline* (CW13), Rudolf Steiner Press, UK 2011.

—, *Original Impulses for the Science of the Spirit* (CW96), Completion Press, Australia 2001.

—, *The Presence of the Dead on the Spiritual Path* (CW154), Anthroposophic Press, USA 1990.

—, *Problems of Society: An Esoteric View, From Luciferic Past to Ahrimanic Future* (CW193), Rudolf Steiner Press, UK 2015.

—, *Reading the Pictures of the Apocalypse* (CW104a), Anthroposophic Press, USA 1991.

—, *The Spiritual Guidance of the Individual and Humanity* (CW15), Anthroposophic Press, USA 1992.

—, *Spiritual Science as a Foundation for Social Forms* (CW199), Anthroposophic Press, USA 1986.

—, *Sprüche, Dichtungen, Mantren, Ergänzungsband: Nachträge, Handschriften* [Proverbs, Poems, Mantras: Supplementary Volume – Addendums, Manuscripts] (GA40a), Rudolf Steiner Verlag, Switzerland 2002.

—, *Study of Man: General Education Course* (CW293), Rudolf Steiner Press, UK 2004.

—, *The Temple Legend and the Golden Legend: Freemasonry and Related Occult Movements* (CW93), Rudolf Steiner Press, UK 1997.

—, *Three Paths to Christ: Experiencing the Supersensible* (CW143), Rudolf Steiner Press, UK 2023.

—, *Truth-Wrought Words* (CW40), Anthroposophic Press, USA 1979.

—, *Understanding Society Through Spiritual-Scientific Knowledge: Social Threefolding, Christ, Lucifer and Ahriman* (CW191), Rudolf Steiner Press, UK 2017.

—, *Universal Spirituality and Human Physicality: Bridging the Divide* (CW202), Rudolf Steiner Press, UK 2014.

—, *The Value of Thinking: For a Cognition that Satisfies the Human Being – The Relationship Between Spiritual Science and Natural Science* (CW164), Rudolf Steiner Press, UK 2023.

—, *Verses and Meditations*, Rudolf Steiner Press, UK 1993.

—, *Vorträge und Kurse über christlich-religiöses Wirken, Bd.3, Vorträge bei der Begründung der Christengemeinschaft* [Lectures and Courses on Christian Religious Work, Volume 3: Lectures at the Founding of the Christian Community] (GA344), Rudolf Steiner Verlag, Switzerland 1994.

Tabarki, Farid, *The End of the Middle: What a Society of Extremes Means for People, Politics and Business*, Warden Press, Holland 2017.

Truman, Harry S., *Memoirs of Harry S. Truman, Vol. 1: Year of Decisions*, Doubleday & Company, USA 1955.

Index

Floris
Books

For news on all our **latest books,**
and to receive **exclusive discounts,**
join our mailing list at:

florisbooks.co.uk/signup

Plus subscribers get a FREE book
with every online order!

We will never pass your details to anyone else.